The Widow's Journey

GRIEF AND RECOVERY

By

Janet B. Wright

Second Edition

ISBN: 1-4392-1612-6

In loving memory of Jim
Husband, Father, Physician,
Naturalist, and Musician

And to our four sons:
Paul, John, Joe, and Steve

Our two grandchildren:
Nolan and Tessa

And
Widows Everywhere

Death be not proud, though some have called thee
Mighty and dreadful, for thou art not so,
....

One short sleep past, we wake eternally.

John Donne

Foreword

Jan and her husband, Dr James J. Wright, lived for many years in a world of gifted sons, books, music, travel, ideas, nature, and helping people in need. They cared deeply for each other.

That world of riches was suddenly destroyed by Jim's heart attack.

In this book Jan, a teacher of English and a student of psychology, has written with rare honesty and insight about her entry into a desolate new world, her survival strategies, and her search for a road toward healing. Her unique self-awareness, her creative mental energy, and her inclusion of other widows' stories combine to provide a valuable guide and support for widows everywhere.

John B. Scofield, M.D.
Clinical Professor of Psychiatry
Indiana University School of Medicine

Introduction

Dear Readers;

When my husband died after so many years together, I was devastated and frightened. I was at a loss as to how I could emotionally and strategically go forward. Nor did I want to. In the beginning, it was all I could do to get up in the morning and face another lonely and agonizing day. The one thing I did initially, on the advice of my sons, was create a journal of what I was experiencing and feeling. They hoped this would ease some of my anxiety and grief. And so, every day, I chronicled my emotions and behavior, which were, at first, unproductive if not destructive.

Somewhere in the fourth or fifth month of my widowhood, I became acquainted with a number of other widows and began to realize that we shared a common bond. They too were in a desolate state of being. In my desire to communicate how well I understood what they were experiencing, I began sharing my journal with them. To my surprise, these widows enthusiastically reported back to me how strongly they related to what I had written and urged me to make my journal accessible to more women. In response to their advice, I wrote and published *The Widow's Journey* and am now offering it to others seeking understanding and help.

My goal, as I wrote the book, was to relate to my readers how I went about the healing process—the many roads I traveled to find peace and stability in my new life. These include my early destructive behavior with alcohol and drugs. But, more importantly, I discuss the many positive avenues I traveled, such as attending a grief group, getting back in touch with nature, trying biofeedback, practicing meditation, designing a memorial album, and numerous other techniques. All of these I discuss in detail, so the reader has a clear idea of what each involved. Included throughout the book are also many helpful suggestions by specialists in the field of grieving and my comments on how helpful these were for me. (Experts in the field of grief can offer a great deal, but they don't seem to be writing for us widows, but for others in their field.) Thus, in my book I attempt to put their words into more understandable context. Finally, I incorporated a number of moving stories told to me by other widows, compelling personal experiences that I will never forget. And I am confident: neither will you.

If you are a widow of short or long standing, I hope this book will touch your heart and perhaps move you to share your narrative with others. By doing so we can help each other. Since listening to many such stories, I now feel a genuine bond with the many, who like us, have lost a loved one. No one else can understand this as we do, so don't hesitate to add your voice. Feel free to do this on my web site: www.The Widows Journey.com.

Janet B. Wright

Acknowledgments

Ironic as it may seem, I want first to acknowledge my husband without whom this book would not have been written. Though I would, of course, rather have him here with me, I am grateful for the many times during my life that he encouraged me to move forward with my personal development. This wonderful man babysat with our four young children many, many evenings for five years while I pursued my master's degree. I will never forget his love and commitment to our family and me.

I have had other teachers in my life: My mother, Marion O'Dowd Bayer, widowed at a young age with three preschool children, taught me how strong a woman can be. The memory of her struggle to earn a living, while seeing to the upbringing of her three girls, has been an inspiration to me in these past six years.

There are not enough words to thank my four sons for their caring and support after my husband died. They were at my side within hours of the tragedy, supported me during the awful days following, and remain very close to this day, especially Paul, who has been my bedrock these past six years. I am grateful to them as well for their support, suggestions and critique of this book. Special thanks must go to Steve, the writer in our family, for his encouragement when I became frustrated, his aid with technical advice when I was faced with computer glitches, and his wonderful photograph for the cover. I must also thank Jay Hilgenberg for coming to my rescue when I needed help with my format. Finally, I so much appreciate the editing advice of my dear friend Margaret G. Dean, Esq..

My gratitude also goes to my brother-in-law, Dr. Thomas L. Wright, for stepping into my sons' and my life at a time when we had lost our captain and desperately needed someone to steer the ship until we regained our emotional stability.

A special thanks also to my friends, who, lovingly and patiently, let me cry on their shoulders and listened to me tell my sad story over and over again. I am further indebted to all those friends who refused to let me remain disconnected from the world at a time when I wanted only isolation. Their notes and emails reminded me that, when I was ready, they were there for me.

Last but not least, I am grateful to Johnella Womack, Yolanda Floreancig, Jane Miller [an alias], Barbara Stephenson, Margaret Anne Ervin, Lois Frye, and Lillian Hall, widows who generously shared their stories for this book, in spite of the pain it caused them to do so.

Janet B. Wright

Table of Contents

1
My Story

In the days and weeks that followed the death of my husband, I was pulled in two directions: On the one hand, I wanted to escape, to crawl into a hole somewhere and hide. On the other, I felt a driving need to share with others, especially my family, what had happened—how my husband had died. Many professionals in the field of bereavement recommend that the widow turn to a trusted friend with whom she can feel at ease and tell her story. Indeed, it is said that a spouse must tell her story a hundred times before finding some measure of relief. I don't know if relief is possible at this point, but it certainly was helpful for me because, in the beginning, and for some time after, the terrible event that I had experienced was not believable. From almost the very beginning of this nightmare, I was in a state of extreme shock, intense emotional pain, and disbelief. After all, how could my husband of forty-three years be gone? What mysterious process transformed this vital human being into a lifeless corpse?

Fortunately, I had relatives and close friends who wanted to be helpful and listened patiently while I pondered these questions and related my story. They allowed me to expose my raw emotions, to cry as much as I needed, and to describe what had happened. That process, at this point in my grieving, was essential to setting me on the path to emotional healing. For some women, however, exposing themselves in such a manner is extremely difficult; yet, it is important to make the effort. Therefore, I will begin by telling you my story, in the hope that it will encourage you to do the same....

The Last Day

It was a beautiful day in Sonoma and our last day of vacation in California. We had a wonderful ten days, visiting two of our sons in Los Angeles, seeing some plays, visiting several museums, and so on. Now we were in Sonoma Valley visiting Jim's sister, Peggy, and her husband, Joe. Easter Sunday, the day before, which we shared with family and friends, had been delightful.

But both Jim and I were looking forward to returning to Indianapolis on Tuesday. It was spring, and we were eager to return to our home, especially our garden, where we had always spent many happy hours working with plants, flowers, trees and shrubs. Jim had a particular interest in wild flowers and indigenous plants, so working with these gave him much pleasure. Indeed, I knew his being in touch with nature nurtured his soul. After a hard day of work, we would sit on the patio, admiring the results of our labors, while we savored a well-earned cocktail.

But we still had a day in Sonoma and decided to drive into town to window shop and purchase a gift for our hosts. We had a lovely day, strolling around the quaint town square, stopping in the exquisite little shops to make a few purchases: Jim pondered over a small brass horse and finally succumbed to the magnificence of its craftsmanship. (He was not an impulsive buyer!) Stopping at an outside café for lunch, Jim offered to order me a glass of wine. I teased him that I was not sure his judgment could be trusted, given the fact he had lost the wine tasting contest the day before!

That evening after dinner with Peg and Joe, we returned to their home to accomplish the unpleasant task of packing all our belongings. As we entered our room, it was obvious that Jim was not feeling well. He had suffered with angina for years, but not to the point of needing medical assistance. As a physician, he was aware of his body and knew how to control these symptoms. But this was different; his breathing sounded congested, and he said he was going to need oxygen. He wanted to wait to see if his condition improved, but I insisted, "No, we're going to the hospital now."

My brother-in-law drove us the few blocks to the emergency room where Jim was taken directly back to a treatment area, while I stayed at the front desk to sign the obligatory papers. By the time I reached my husband's side, he was in serious breathing distress and was being given oxygen, morphine, and I'm not sure what else. He was clammy to the touch so I kept cold compresses on his forehead, while the medical staff continued to work diligently over him. It was a relief to observe that the staff was so competent, as I felt completely helpless to do anything except try to comfort my husband. This is true, I suspect, of anyone who finds herself in such a situation.

In approximately thirty minutes, Jim's breathing became almost normal, and he began to relax. Now the discussion of what had happened, and what was next came into play. The staff believed my husband had suffered a heart attack and needed to be transferred to a cardiac hospital in a nearby town for further evaluation and treatment. This seemed like the obvious thing to do at this juncture, and neither Jim nor I protested or even questioned the wisdom of this decision. The crisis seemed to have passed and we all considered the present danger over. Tomorrow we would find out what the cardiologists believed should be the next step. We assumed that would mean facing difficult decisions about surgery, but at this point, both Jim and I were feeling relieved enough to do some gentle teasing with each other. (I don't know how other wives handle such critical moments, but I didn't want Jim to know how terribly worried I really was. That would only make the situation worse for him, and would accomplish nothing positive, to be sure.)

Late that night, when we reached the cardiac facility, I rode up on the elevator with the medics and Jim. I asked him if he had ever ridden in an ambulance before. He gave me that devilish look of his and said, "Not as a patient!" Those were to be the last words he was ever to say to me. The medics rolled him into a room, where we were met by nurses who shooed my brother-in-law and me out, sending us to the waiting room until they could get Jim settled in. Though I was eager to stay at his side, her request seemed reasonable, so we reluctantly retired to the waiting room. Not ten minutes later, the hospital intercom announced a Code Blue. Knowing instinctively it was for Jim, I jumped up and ran to his room. But the nurse met me in the hall and quite emphatically told me to go back to the waiting room and let her look after Jim's needs. I knew she was right, and so I obeyed her command and returned to the loneliness of the waiting room.

It was at this time (though it was 4:00 AM) that I knew I needed to contact our sons. I had thought about it earlier in the emergency room, but the physician in charge recommended I wait until I had discussed Jim's condition with the cardiologists. Now, however, the foreboding was palpable, so I started making those dreaded calls. Though my heart was pounding, and I was overwhelmed with a powerful sense of doom, I stayed focused. I had two goals: first, to reach the children before Jim died, so they would have a chance to adjust to what I knew my next call would surely be. Second, I wanted to sound calm, in control, so they didn't suffer the added anxiety of worrying about me. One by one, I gave them the terrible news that their father had suffered a heart attack and was in grave condition. Nothing I had ever done in my life was more difficult than that!

Not long thereafter, two cardiologists joined us in the waiting room to bring the inevitable, though still appalling news, that Jim had not made it—that their thirty minutes of attempts at resuscitation had failed. I wanted to shout at them that *they* were the ones who had not made it. After all, *they* were the specialists. My husband was in their capable hands. Instead, I merely said, "I want to see him."

As I walked up to the bed, I was struck by how peaceful Jim looked—like a little boy tucked in for the night, sleeping soundly. Except for a small tube still in his mouth, he looked fine. I bent over and touched him. His arms were already cold, but his face was warm and I kissed his forehead, over and over again. A priest appeared and began to perform the last rites. It was all so surreal. I couldn't think clearly. My hands folded, I stood over Jim, quietly saying The *Lord's Prayer* along with the priest. I felt like a confused and frightened little girl in the presence of a force much greater than myself, of which I had no understanding and over which I had no control.

After the priest left, I stayed with Jim a while longer, still kissing him on the forehead. I didn't want to leave him there, alone in a strange place, but I had no choice. As my brother-in-law and I exited the hospital, I noticed that the sun was coming up over the hills. It was Tuesday morning—the day Jim and I were scheduled to return to our beloved home....

Your Story

Every woman's story is different, of course, and telling it will be extremely painful, but you will experience some emotional release in doing so. The nightmare is running through your brain continuously anyway; it will help ease your anguish to finally put voice to all those thoughts. Be sure, therefore, to choose a sympathetic listener with whom you can feel completely comfortable. Such a person or persons will make it easier for you to give expression to your feelings. If you have no one who fits this profile, call your place of worship or a hospice and inquire if they have anyone who can help you with this process. I am confident that they do, and I know you will be glad you did so.

If you can find no one with whom you can relate, or at this point cannot bring yourself to communicate your story to another human being, write it down, or tell your story into a tape recorder. The advantage of this is that you can read or listen to your story whenever you are inclined to do so. In a way, it *is* like telling your story a hundred times. In addition, this record is a testimonial to the man you loved and can be saved by you and family members as a significant document to be preserved, not unlike a birth, marriage, or death certificate. Whatever your choice may be, find the courage to give your story the light of day. Keeping it buried inside your heart will only exacerbate your torment. Following are the stories of three women who found the courage to relate their experiences.

Jonella's Story

It was a beautiful summer day, and Ike and I were looking forward to spending the afternoon together, but first he had some errands to run. He decided to take his bike rather than the car, which was not unusual for him. But when he didn't return after a few hours, I became somewhat anxious. An hour later, I received a call from the hospital emergency room telling me that Ike had been hit by a car. I was alone and breathless; I didn't know what to do. I called a friend who took me to the hospital where a doctor and a chaplain met us and told me that Ike did not make it...It was the saddest day of my life.

Lois's Story

Like Jonella, Lois lost her husband in a terrible accident:

It was ten o'clock at night, and Larry was due home at any time. Then the phone rang; Larry was calling to say his car was overheating and he was worried that it would break down...would I meet him and follow him home. Tired and a bit frustrated, I grabbed my keys and headed out to rendezvous with him at a restaurant parking lot where he was waiting.

Upon my arrival, I suggested that we leave the car and return the next morning to retrieve it. He said that he thought we could make it home if we drove slowly and stopped several times along the way. With that, we headed home, my following right behind Larry's car. We did have to stop three or four times on this journey, because the car kept over heating. Each time, I begged him to leave the car. It was on our last stop that I again climbed into Larry's car and we sat there talking, while we waited for the engine to cool. It was then that he turned to me and said, 'Lois, I loved you yesterday, I love you today, and I will love you always.' Those were the last words that I ever heard from him.

When we reached a road near our home (an unlighted area) we encountered two very slow moving vehicles ahead of us. Black smoke was rolling out of my husband's car as he overtook them. By the time I was able to pass the cars, my husband was out of view. Assuming that Larry was up ahead of me, I continued home, expecting to find him already there. But he wasn't. At this point I was filled with anxiety and headed back out to retrace my route, assuming his car had broken down, and I had missed him, given the lack of light in the area. When I reached the place where we had overtaken the cars, the road was blocked with police cars, an ambulance and a fire truck. I parked my car and ran frantically toward what I now could see was Larry's car crushed into a tree. But a fireman stopped me and escorted me to a police car where he told me to wait. It was a lonely, frightening wait... Only later would I learn that Larry died on impact. No one was ever able to determine the exact cause of the accident. Larry was only forty-four years old.

Margaret Anne's Story

Not all widows lost their husbands in a sudden event. Many women painfully watched as their husbands struggled for years with an illness. Margaret Anne is one such woman. For three years, off and on, Gene had to have dialysis, which he chose to do at home with Margaret Anne's help. She was a nurse, but had not done this kind of procedure before:

It was very stressful for both of us because of concerns with blood pressure drops and spikes, but the most tense situations involved power outages in the neighborhood during storms. This happened several times, and I would have to manually keep the machine going in order to keep Gene's blood from clotting.

Finally, Gene received a kidney transplant, which was truly a gift from God. For awhile our lives were pretty good, until I discovered that he was suffering from jaundice:

After having blood tests that showed Gene's liver was abnormal, surgeons performed a Whipple procedure. The diagnosis was pancreatic cancer, which had spread into the ducts. The surgeons told us that the surgery would give Gene some time and comfort, but that there was no cure for pancreatic cancer.

During Gene's last hospitalization in November, the doctors said that all that could be done had been done. At Gene's request we chose Hospice to intervene when we would need them, but I would be his primary caregiver.

Just before Christmas a feeding tube was inserted, but after a week Gene asked that it be removed as it was 'bothersome.' We knew this meant that he was ready to die as he took nothing but water from that point on.

On Christmas day our children came to spend what they knew was their last Christmas with their father. It was a very quiet day with music playing softly in the background and everyone sharing family stories.

Gene died peacefully on January 10. It seemed impossible that he was no longer with me. With the help of my children, grandchildren, friends and my faith, I would find my way —a new way.

Margaret Anne's courage and commitment to the man she loved is such an inspiring story. There are so many other women who have suffered similarly. Every widow has a story, and it needs to be shared for her sake and for all the other widows who can identify with it and relate it to her own. Perhaps hearing one woman's story will help others tell theirs.

2
Need To Know

Jim was dead. I was miserable and confused. At the time of his death, I had not asked the doctors any questions. I was in shock, and besides nothing they could have said would have changed the terrible truth. I knew he died of a heart attack, but I wanted to understand exactly what had happened to his heart. Why now? What was different this time from all the other times he had suffered angina? When the time was suitable, I turned to my son, John, a physician, to explain to me in a manner that I could understand. I asked him to do it in writing, so I could read it as often as I wished in order to better assimilate the information. Here is what he wrote:

Dear Mom,

I know the journey of healing for most of us is one of searching for truth—philosophical, spiritual, psychological, and an assortment of other truths. Part of this journey for you is gaining some understanding of the medical facts surrounding Dad's death. As it happened, Dad died of a heart attack, one of the leading causes of death in the industrialized world. I'll try to explain what happens:

The heart is a large muscle whose job it is to pump blood to all the organs in the body so that they can use the oxygen provided in the blood to function properly. The heart muscles squeeze in synchrony about sixty times a minute over your entire life. In order for the entire muscle to squeeze in a coordinated fashion, there is an electrical conduction system that rapidly communicates across the entire heart so each muscle fiber "knows" when to fire.

Both the muscle of the heart and the conduction system of the heart depend on blood themselves provided by several arteries called the coronary arteries. Without a constant flow of blood, the conduction system and the muscles of the heart cannot function. It is in these arteries where a heart attack starts, and the process begins as early as our teenage years.

Coronary arteries, like the rest of the arteries of our system, are soft tubes perfectly designed to deliver blood to our heart— at least when we are born. Over time, however, these arteries slowly "harden." More specifically, substances flowing in our blood (e.g. cholesterol) are laid into the walls of the arteries making them less smooth, and therefore more difficult for blood to get through.

Time is the major contributor to hardening of these arteries, a process called arteriosclerosis. Your genes may make you more or less susceptible as well. You cannot control these factors. However, there are many factors that you can control such as not smoking, watching your diet, and getting regular exercise.

Eventually, the coronary arteries become so hardened that it is very difficult for blood to get to the heart. At this point, a person is at high risk for blood in a coronary artery to clot completely off. If this happens (as it usually does) it results in damage to the heart, which is a heart attack. If only a small amount of muscle is damaged, a person may just have some chest pain or shortness of breath and may recover quite well.

There are two ways a heart attack can cause death. If the coronary artery that gets blocked is large enough, so much heart muscle will be damaged that it simply cannot pump any longer. Without blood, the organs of the body cannot function. A person will become short of breath, lose consciousness, or both, and very soon the heart will simply stop pumping.

The second problem that can occur with a heart attack is a disruption in the electrical system that the heart uses to synchronize the muscle fibers. If a coronary artery is blocked that feeds blood to an important branch or communication point, the entire system can be disrupted. This is similar to any communication system. For example, if the telephone wire to your house is knocked out, only your telephone (or a few muscle fibers) stops working. If the telephone company headquarters is knocked out, the whole system breaks down. Similarly, when a vital part of the conduction system is blocked the heart muscles contract, but without any coordination it becomes essentially useless. All blood flow to the body stops, and the person becomes immediately unconscious and is essentially dead. This is when paddles can be used to "shock" the heart, hoping it begins beating again. Sometimes this works, often it doesn't. This is what happened to Dad.

I hope this helps in your search for understanding of what happened to Dad. All this happened so fast, that Dad did not suffer in the least. Hopefully, this will be of some comfort to all of us.

Love,
John

As a widow, you may not have a need to understand exactly what happened to bring about your husband's death. But if you do want to know, that is your right. When you are emotionally prepared to concentrate on such matters, make an appointment with your husband's attending physician and request that he take time to explain to you, in layman's language, the circumstances of your husband's illness and death. Some of this you will already know, but it will not hurt for your doctor to review this with you. Have someone accompany you to this meeting so he or she can take notes and ask questions that you may neglect to ask. You will have many questions after the death of your husband, and gaining information may very well help you deal with your grief.

3
Planning the Funeral

All of us have viewed movies with scenes of funeral rites, especially in the old country where the family prepares the body for burial, lays the loved one out in the parlor, and invites friends in to bid a final farewell. This seems completely foreign to us today, but I wonder if it isn't a much more personal process than the rituals we now follow. Catherine Sanders, in her book *Grief the Mourning After*, makes a convincing argument that rituals are an important part of the grieving process, because they supply the family and community with "a deeper meaning to life" (250). I agree. Was not my husband someone I loved and cherished? Someone I admired and respected? Could I simply call a funeral director and turn these final, crucial moments of my husband's time on this earth over to a stranger's discretion? But what to do? Where do my sons and I begin? With grief raging, we blindly plunged into the process.

For those of you who are reading this before your loved one dies, I hope it will be of help to you in preparing yourself practically and psychologically for what you must face. It is for this reason that I relate my experience:

Though we had discussed it on several occasions, my husband and I had made no concrete plans for our eventual deaths (after all, what was the hurry?). Consequently, every decision, down to the last detail, had to be made at this difficult time. Here I was, burying the man I loved—the man with whom I had spent most of my adult life. And my sons were burying their father with whom they had been extremely close. In this devastating emotional state, and with our vast lack of experience in this arena, we had to face the excruciatingly arduous task of planning the funeral.

One decision I had already made—the funeral would be a private one. My emotional state was such that I knew I could not face a public event. Jim's active life in the community would have normally meant a large number of people that my sons and I would have to relate to and, in some instances, comfort. This decision for privacy, I knew, would possibly not be received favorably by everyone. After all, they had cared about Jim too and would want to express their sympathies. But I believe funerals are not unlike weddings in that the people most intimately involved must choose what is best for them. And I knew I had all I could do to cope with my own pain and that of my sons. Besides, Jim was a quiet, reserved man— not one partial to public events. Thus, I was confident that he would have approved of a private funeral with only his family present.

With this decision made, I thought we had crossed a huge hurdle, but I would discover to the contrary when my sons and I met with the funeral directors, in what turned out to be an ordeal like none any of us had ever experienced. I don't remember all the details; there were so many. In what took hours, we went through innumerable issues one by one: coroner's report, number of death certificates (how did I know how many death certificates I needed?), information for the newspapers, flowers, music, clothes for Jim and on and on. It was overwhelming. It was grim. It was painful.

In all fairness, the funeral directors were quite helpful and very patient with us. They and we were after the same thing: Jim's funeral and burial. But for them it was just business as usual. For us, it was the last act we would ever perform for the man we had loved so dearly. Therefore, coming from such different perspectives, the directors appeared cold and void of any feeling, which only added to our own sense of wretchedness.

Because the funeral arrangements were so driven by business, my sons and I were more than ever determined that Jim's service would be a reflection of our love for him and our respect for the many significant contributions he had made during his life. I was later to read in Sander's book the following:

> The ceremony selected will, in itself, be a form of
> memorial that provides an opportunity to offer respect to
> the deceased. The more personally meaningful the ritual,
> the more important it becomes to the bereaved (253).

So our instincts were pointing us in the right direction, even though we were not aware of it at the time.

Our first decision was to ask a psychiatrist, Dr. Alan Smetzer, who had worked with my husband for many years to give the eulogy. We wanted him to reflect back on Jim's twenty years as the executive and medical director of the largest mental health center in the state. Next, we searched successfully for a priest who would give the kind of spiritual tone we thought appropriate for this ritual. In addition, because Jim was such a fine pianist we gathered together some of the work he had put on tape, so we could play Jim's own music at the funeral. We designed two photo displays: one depicting Jim's life from preschool to the present and the other of his beautiful garden. Finally, we designed a program using lovely photographs that Jim had taken of his garden. (I later sent these programs to out-of-town friends and distant relatives to announce Jim's death.)

With heavy hearts, all was accomplished in only a few short days. It is a mystery how one can do so much planning in such a state of grief. But there was no time to think about that in the middle of such a flurry of activity. Our hearts were indeed heavy, but our minds were like steel traps. The grieving would come soon enough.

If you can make plans before a death in the family, by all means, do so. It will make the process much less traumatic for survivors. Moreover, it gives you the opportunity to research various options such as funeral homes, cemeteries, religious affiliations, and so on. The expenses of a funeral can vary greatly, and it is much more likely that you can find a more reasonable one when you are not in a state of grief and anxiety. If this is not possible, as it often is not, turn to your place of worship for guidance. Or seek the assistance of a close relative or friend. Another possibility: I recently stumbled over an Internet site (www.lutheranlife.ca) that walks the family through the entire planning process, including a cost analysis breakdown. I would have liked to have seen this when we began our planning, if only as a guideline to aid us in such unfamiliar territory.

4
The Funeral

When the day of the funeral arrived, I picked a large bouquet of flowers from the garden to put on Jim's casket. They were lovely spring flowers that he had grown with his own hands. We also brought baskets of ferns from the garden patio to flank the coffin. We wanted, once again, for the funeral service to be as personal as possible. Using Jim's own flowers seemed one more way to accomplish this.

At the hospital, after Jim died, I had the opportunity to spend some time alone with him and so was somewhat prepared to view his body in the coffin. But our sons had not, and I was concerned about how they would react to seeing him in this manner. As it turned out, all of us felt as though we were not really viewing the man we knew, but only a shell of him. His spirit was not in that coffin. This seemed to ease the shock for all of us.

Most men are buried in business suits, but I wanted Jim dressed in more casual clothes, something I had always felt he looked particularly attractive in. With this in mind, I chose a white shirt and a navy v-neck cashmere sweater, which he had worn often. I also chose one of his favorite ties: one depicting the *Canterbury Tales*, which I had bought for him in a museum shop many years before. Jim had always been more comfortable in semi-casual attire, and I wanted him in that now.

Because we had chosen not to have a public viewing, the personal good-byes were not prolonged. We along with Jim's siblings said our farewells before the beginning of the service. During this time, our sons took turns playing the grand piano, which had been provided for this purpose. Each son chose to play something personal between him and his father. This was sad to hear but beautiful and meaningful. After they finished, the tapes of Jim's own piano playing were played and continued in the background throughout the ceremony.

Dr. Smetzer then gave the eulogy. He spoke of Jim as "a skilled administrator, a talented psychiatric clinician, an experienced teacher, and an accomplished musician." He praised Jim's "creativity, his enthusiasm, his perseverance." He expressed his appreciation for Jim's talent in creating "an atmosphere of caring and recognition of hard work in an overworked public agency" like Midtown Mental Health Center. In conclusion he said: "He was a good man and a fierce friend. We will always keep him in our hearts."

When he finished, the priest spoke, suggesting the lovely possibility that God needed Jim in heaven as pianist for His choir of angels. Before closing his eulogy, the priest read each family member's farewell to Jim.

After the service, we proceeded to the gravesite for final blessings and brief words from the priest. The flowers I brought from Jim's garden were again placed on his coffin, and it was time to say our final farewells. I chose not to watch the coffin lowered into the ground; it was simply something I could not bear to see. But Joe and Steve decided to stay and assure themselves that their father was safely placed in the ground, their way of completing the process in which they had been so intimately involved these last few days.

Yet, I did not want the day to end on such a somber note. I wanted to celebrate Jim's life in a place that had been such a joy for him. With this in mind, I had the family gather in Jim's garden for a stroll through this beautiful place, pointing out many of his favorite specimens. After this, we convened on the patio where we toasted Jim with his cocktail of choice—the Manhattan. I knew my husband would approve of such a conclusion to the day, as this was precisely how we had ended many, many of our days together.

The funeral rites were now at an end. Curiously, I had the strangest sense that I had participated in something extremely significant. In my subsequent readings I ran across a work by the authors Hine and Foster who described such rituals as "participation in the workings of the universe." Yes, I thought, we had indeed connected with something greater than ourselves on that sad, sad day.

When planning your loved one's funeral, remember that you and those close to you are the only ones you need to be concerned about. The others will take care of themselves. Furthermore, on the day of your loved one's funeral, feel free to follow your instincts regarding your behavior. Do not be concerned with what others may think. If you need to cry, do so. If you are uncomfortable with others seeing you grieve, that's fine too. If you wish to keep family and friends close to you, invite them back to your home and spend time with them. Listen carefully to your feelings. Let them lead you through this day. Those around you will take their cues from you and do as you wish. Your needs are paramount. Let them be so...

Tony's Funeral

When my husband died, my sons and I turned to the Catholic Church that Jim and I had once attended. We found the priest kind and helpful in planning the funeral service, but because we had not been members of the church for many years, he did not know us personally and could not possibly relate to our family in a manner that might have been of some comfort.

This was not true of Yolanda's experience when she buried her husband. Tony had been a member of this same Catholic Church for many, many years and had a large number of friends who also attended this church. Consequently, these people came to her aid immediately and helped plan the service. The Knights of Columbus held a prayer service at the funeral home, and the women's association hosted a memorial dinner for all who wished to attend.

Yolanda's experience with the church, I have found, is not unusual. Church members, no matter what affiliation, help their members through this most difficult of times.

Whatever experience you have had with the funeral process, the time will come when you will want to consider other ways to continue to honor your husband. Such activities will be comforting to you and your family. Here are a few ideas to consider, some of which may appeal to you:

1. Write a poem describing what you loved about him, or write a letter to him saying the same thing. Keep it in a special place.
2. Light a candle once a day or once a week in his honor.
3. Design a memorial album that includes your favorite pictures, letters, anything that reminds you of your life together. Return to it from time to time and just browse through it.
4. Draw a picture of what comes into your mind when you think of him. Frame it, or add it to your album.
5. Visit his grave. Bring a flower from your garden. Sit and talk to him about your feelings at this time in your grieving process.
6. Have a prayer said for him in your place of worship.
7. When you come together as a family, make a toast in his memory.

8. Donate to his favorite charity.
9. Plant a garden in his memory. Place a stone with his name on it in the center.
10. Write a biography of his life and present it to your children. Or write the story of your life together.

As you can see, the possibilities for honoring your loved one are endless. Use your imagination and come up with what is unique and comforting for you.

5
Life After Death

Do you believe that the spirit survives in some form after the body dies? I do. Perhaps this is wishful thinking on my part, but it has sustained me through this most difficult time of my life. Furthermore, I suspect it is what will keep me going for the rest of my life. Do I have proof? Of course not. I certainly wish I did; I could make everyone's life easier. I would spread the good news far and wide. I am not alone in my thinking, however, as there seems to be a growing interest in the subject of life after death in all facets of society. Many have certainly seen John Edward's show "Crossing Over" on television. His popularity is a testament to the number of people who are curious about life after death. But Edward is a medium, not a scientist, and certainly has some detractors.

Not true of the late Dr. Elisabeth Kubler-Ross, a respected psychiatrist and an expert in the field of death and dying, who did a good deal of research over the years on the subject. After many years of working with the dying, she became convinced that when the spirit leaves the body, it becomes part of another form of energy that lives on. As a result of her observations, she began a life-long study in an attempt to verify what she strongly suspected to be true. As her research progressed, she became more convinced than ever after studying people "from different cultural and religious backgrounds, including Eskimos, Buddhists, Protestants, Catholics, Jews and several people without any religious identification, including a few who call themselves agnostics or atheists" (498). She and her colleagues found that all their subjects, no matter how they "died" underwent very similar experiences, which they related to physicians and relatives upon resuscitation. All of this has now been documented. If you are interested in this subject, Kubler-Ross's books, as well as the works of many others in this field, are readily available in your bookstore or library.

Perhaps I bring up the respected Dr. Kubler-Ross because I feel defensive about discussing a subject that so many will be quick to criticize. It is, after all, embarrassing to speak of issues that one cannot substantiate. "Where's the proof?" skeptics will say. Indeed, I learned in graduate school to support my statements with facts, and in my many years of teaching high school English, I insisted that my students do the same. But the experiences I will share with you below cannot be supported with "facts." You can put whatever value on them you wish. I do believe, however, that we all have experiences that we cannot explain rationally, and we usually shrug them off because they don't pass the test of our five senses. But what if we have other senses of which we are unaware? I believe we all have experiences that suggest something we cannot explain. Wouldn't it be interesting if we gave them more consideration? Would it not also be fascinating if we could hear from others, who have had inexplicable experiences as well? In the grief-counseling group (which I was later to attend), many of the participants related stories that convinced me that they had, indeed, been involved in such phenomena. I have had only a few experiences of this kind, but they were enough to leave a lasting impression on me.

For example, three weeks before my husband died, I was preparing to join him in California for a two-week vacation. He was already out West doing some consulting work and I was to meet him in a few days. Typical of many of us before we leave on holiday, I was running around trying to get house and garden in tip top shape, so things would be looking their best when we returned. Then, the day before I left, as I came into the house after a hard day's work in the garden, an inexplicable thought went through my mind: "See, you can manage this house by yourself if you have to." I was astounded by this seemingly irrational thought. I had no reason to think such a thing. Why would I have to manage the house by myself? I brushed it off as an aberration of the brain. But three weeks later, after I buried Jim, I remembered that day and that thought, and I now believe this was meant as a heads up for me, but at the time, I didn't get it.

Another profound experience happened to me about a month after Jim died. When I was at one of my lowest points, I begged my husband to give me some sign that he was still with me, that I simply could not bear this pain without him. That afternoon, I gathered up the courage to walk down to the street to check the mailbox, a chore I did not accomplish every day. As I stood at the box, a friend and neighbor, Joyce Young, walked over to say hello and see how I was getting along. In a matter of minutes, a car stopped in front of us and I thought: "Dear God, please don't let this be another well-meaning neighbor stopping to express his condolences." Instead, it was a sweet-looking, little old man who had lost his way. I was not enthusiastic about getting involved, but I felt sorry for this poor, lost soul. He had a phone number, so I retrieved a portable phone, called his party who gave us directions, and sent him on his way. He no sooner started up his car when he stopped abruptly, got out of his car, and walked straight toward me, handed me a small item and said: "I want you to have this." It was a tiny, hand crafted, angel! Now, I have lived in this house for thirty-five years and given directions to uncountable numbers of people; yet, no one has ever before given me a gift, let alone an angel. I was convinced, and am still convinced, that Jim sent that angel to let me know he was, indeed, still with me.

But the story doesn't end there: Six months later, when I told Joyce what that angel had meant to me, she told me this:

That day, when you came out with the phone in your hand, you tried to hand it to me, I guess because you didn't feel up to dealing with the problem. I walked toward you to take the phone, when I heard a voice in my head that was so strong I turned around to see if someone was standing behind me. The voice said: 'Let Jan do it.' I heard this twice and decided you had to make that call. Now that I know your experience that day, I am sure it was Jim telling me to let you make the call. I guess so that the man would give you the angel and not me.

Still another incident that made a tremendous impression on me occurred soon after I had some disturbing thoughts that maybe Jim had never loved me, that I had just imagined it. I knew that these feelings were common with new widows, but they distressed me just the same. Of course, I revealed these feelings to no one. Then, a week later I received this email from my son Steve:

Mom,

I've been meaning to tell you about a dream I had recently, but haven't told you sooner— it's just that it's on the intense side, and I wasn't exactly sure when to bring it up, so I decided to write it out for you. Of course, I'm still dreaming about Dad a lot. In general, (and it's a common theme) he doesn't speak. Mostly because he can't, it seems, but in a way, partly because he doesn't need to.

Anyway, I had this dream that Dad and I were in the rec room. I was sitting at the desk at the old Apple computer that you and Dad bought us for Christmas. Dad was sitting in a folding chair next to the desk, wearing his brown suit without the jacket...tie and shirt a little messy as if he had just gotten home from work.

After sitting in silence for a moment, I said to him that I knew he couldn't speak, but asked him if he could type something on the computer...if that would work. Just then, I looked up at the screen, and next to the blinking cursor was written: 'Tell your

mother that I love her.' That was it...it was a fast dream with
only a few clear images.

Pretty intense, huh?

Love,
Steve

Steve didn't know about the private thoughts that had been plaguing me regarding Jim's love; consequently, the significance of that dream for me was profound. Had Jim been aware of my foolish thoughts and sent that message through our son to put my mind at ease?

My son, Paul, also dreams quite frequently about his father. He told me that "*Dad* comes to me often in my dreams, but never says anything, just stands there calmly." His interpretation is that Jim wants to let him know that his "Dad is still around and watching over me."

Still another unusual experience involved my son Joe. I'll let him tell the story in his own words:

A few months after my dad died, my mother and I undertook the painful
task of sorting through many of his belongings. What should be kept?
What should be thrown away? What should be donated? These questions
were anything but straightforward for us, still in the acute, emotional
aftermath of his death.

I ended up sorting through his neckties first. There was one in particu-
lar I wanted to keep: It was his "Scream" tie, which had an image of
Munch's work, the haunting painting of a person screaming with his
hands raised to his face. Dad wore it as his mischievous silent protest
when he had to attend particularly long, non-productive meetings. We
laughed about it multiple times. So it was important for me to find it and
save it.

With his many, many ties now laid out on the bed, I began searching.
After a cursory search provided no success, I put all the ties in a pile on
one side of the bed and carefully moved the ties one-by-one to the other
side, but no "Scream" tie. Did I miss it somewhere else? I looked in his
closet, around the room, and in the drawers. No more ties. So I started
through the pile another time, examining each one and placing it aside.
Again I created a new pile, but found no "Scream." Stepping away from
the bed in disgust, I was ready to give up.

Moments later, my mother called to me from the kitchen. Dinner was
ready. As we ate, I expressed frustration with my inability to locate the tie.
She assured me that it was in there somewhere, unless, that is, one of my

brothers had taken it. But after we had finished eating, while mom cleared our dishes, I decided to return to the task. Walking through the door, my eyes scanned the room. That's when I saw it.

On the floor, a few feet from the bed lay the "Scream" tie, facing up. I could not believe my own eyes, because I know that tie was not on the floor when I left the room, and it was too far away from the bed to have simply fallen. It made no sense to me. Still stunned, I went back to the kitchen with the tie in hand to report this astounding moment to my mother, who seemed less astonished than I. She said Dad had helped me find it.

One final personal experience I will share with you because I was so moved by it:

I had been working in the garden one afternoon and suddenly noticed that I was walking with a very strange gait. Instead of walking straight, I was walking in curves! I tested myself to be sure it wasn't my imagination, but found I could not walk a straight line. My head felt rather strange, so I decided to lie down and see if the malady would pass. It did not. By this time it was 7:00 P.M. on a Saturday night. I did not want to bother my family physician on a weekend night, and I knew my son John (the physician) was gone for the weekend with his wife, so I decided the prudent thing to do was to go to the emergency room in case I was having a stroke. To make a long story short, they kept me for observation for twenty-four hours, found nothing wrong with me and sent me home, after I promised that I would see my own physician for a follow-up. I was annoyed that I had put myself and the medical staff through what was obviously a waste of time.

When I arrived home, I was exhausted (one doesn't sleep in emergency rooms) and fell into bed. But I couldn't sleep. For several hours my mind kept repeating these same words over and over and over again: "Check your medicine," "Check your medicine," "Check your medicine." I was tired and irritated. Finally, I jumped out of bed and shouted out loud (as if talking to someone): "Alright damit, I'll check my medicine!" I knew what medicine I was supposed to check: It was a prescription I had just refilled the day before. Stomping out to the kitchen, I grabbed my glasses and retrieved the medicine. As I read the label on the bottle, I discovered to my astonishment that the prescription had been filled incorrectly—the dosage the pharmacist had given me was for twice what I was supposed to be taking! (The following day my physician agreed that the overdose indeed is what had caused my symptoms.) Never before have I had a problem with medications, so the thought had certainly not occurred to me that medicine was an issue in this case. But it *would* have occurred to my husband. I believe it was his spirit that was nagging me to check my medicine!

Lillian's Dream

Dreams seem to play an important part in our lives, though we usually don't pay much attention to them—except during critical times. Lillian had such a dream, but at the time did not understand its significance. This is what she told me:

I had a wonderful dog named Molly who was a delight to both my husband and me. She was loving, active, and entertaining. A favorite of ours for sure. Sadly, we lost her one October after many years of mutual pleasure. The following March I had a dream about her and, even in my dream, was so pleased to see her again. But she was not the playful Molly I had known; instead, she was very sad. She took me out to the garden and stood with my husband on one side, while I remained on the other, and she said to me, 'We are all in the garden, but we are on different sides.'

At the time I was so delighted to have such a vivid dream of Molly that I didn't think anything about what she said. The next day I related my dream to my husband, as I knew he too would be interested in hearing about Molly. The next night, David died in his sleep. (He was forty-seven and in seemingly good health.)

It was only later, after the funeral, that I remembered my dream, and I knew Molly had been trying to warn me.

My Mother's Dream

Lillian's story reminded me of one my mother told me many years ago:

One night I dreamed of my mother, who had been dead for several years. She was very distressed and was rushing around trying to get my sister and brothers in one place because she had something urgent to tell us. Mother's anxious state made the dream a disturbing one, and I told my husband about it the next day... That very week he was killed in an automobile accident. Then I knew what my mother was trying to tell me.

The more stories I hear like the above, the more certain I am of the significance of dreams in our lives. And I am convinced that these are not exceptions that prove some kind of rule. I have spoken with too many people who have had similar experiences, who have been moved to relate them but only when they felt it was "safe" to do so, when they felt they would not be viewed as unbalanced. It seems to me that we should all be humble enough to at least consider the possibility that there are some things beyond our capacity to know. And in such cases, why not give them the light of day?

If it is any comfort to other laymen like me, even scientists speculate when they find themselves grappling for truths that seem beyond their reach. I found *Scientific American's* special issue of September 2002 on "A Matter of TIME" fascinating. It contains a series of articles, mostly by physicists, discussing the concept of time, in an attempt to define what time really is. The articles are numerous and varied, but as it relates to our question here of life after death, I was interested in Dr. Paul Davies statement of past and future as fixed. "Physicists," he says, "prefer to think of time as laid out in its entirety—a timescape, analogous to a landscape—with all past and future events located there together...." He goes on to speculate: "And what if science were able to explain away the flow of time? Perhaps we would no longer fret about the future or grieve for the past. Worries about death might become as irrelevant as worries about birth....the sense of urgency that attaches to so much of human activity might evaporate....for the past, present and future would literally be things of the past" (42/47).

My point is this: if scientists can surmise about possibilities beyond their knowledge, why can we not do the same? There is much we do not know and cannot prove. Should that stop us from considering the possibilities and gaining comfort from them? I don't think so.

6
Exile

Before and during the funeral rituals, I was too preoccupied to seriously entertain the fact that I would soon have to face life alone. During the funeral I had people around me and there was much to be done. But then everyone left. One by one, my sons reluctantly returned to their out-of-state homes and jobs. Now was the time for me to face the horrific truth: my partner in life was gone forever. I must now face life, all of it, without him, without his support, his advice, his companionship, and his love. I was devastated. I was lost. I was truly alone for the first time in my life, and I didn't have a clue what to do next. Thus, I chose to escape.

Later, I would come to realize that many of my new coping mechanisms were destructive. Isolation, alcohol, drugs, excessive eating, were obviously dangerous. But even if I had considered this to be true at the time, I would not have cared. All I wanted was to be free of pain, and to that end I began to live my days in exile and abusive behavior. I had sent word out to all who knew me that I wanted no visitations, no calls, no flowers, no letters—nothing. Except for my sons, who called me every evening, I had little contact with the outside world. And that was exactly the way I wanted it. Everyone respected my wishes, though I knew few understood. Nor did I, really. I simply succumbed to my feelings. Much later, I was to read the following, which explained what I was going through during this time:

> It is important for the bereaved and their loved ones to understand that this period of mourning is by and large a hibernation time, a holding pattern in which the natural function is to find meaning in the loss, to let go. If this step were more fully understood, the bereaved would feel far less fear and anxiety. Understanding the purpose of this withdrawal will not necessarily reduce the despair, sadness, and sorrow felt because of missing someone who is deeply loved, but it will supply a measure of faith and hope, which promises that healing will occur eventually (228 Sanders).

In those early days of my hibernation, fear was one of my strongest emotions. I was afraid of everything: the phone, the mail, the doorbell, my neighbors, anything or anyone that might demand something of me.

I didn't want to read condolence letters, nor did I wish to speak with anyone offering condolences. This terrible state of fear, in which I found myself, convinced me that I was completely incapable of surviving on my own. Ironically, I had always perceived myself and had been perceived by others, as a fairly strong woman. Now, I felt like an injured child. At this point, I counted it a success if I put my feet on the floor in the morning and made it out to the kitchen for a cup of instant coffee.

If you find yourself in this state of mind, let me offer you some consolation. In Pema Chodron's work *When Things Fall Apart*, she says:

> Fear is a universal experience. Even the smallest insect
> feels it. We wade in the tidal pools and put our finger near
> the soft, open bodies of sea anemones and they close up.
> Everything spontaneously does that. It's not a terrible thing
> that we feel fear when faced with the unknown. It is part of
> being alive (1-2).

The metaphor of the sea anemone suited my situation perfectly, for, like this creature of the sea, I had closed up as tightly as I could manage to do so, as I am sure you have as well. But that's okay. We're in touch with the universe. Less poetic, but just as profound is Catherine Sanders' statement on fear and grief:

> .... in the early phases of grief, when the realization dawns
> for the first time that death is final and that the loved
> person is gone forever, the bereaved often feels panic—a
> fear so intense that it seems over-powering (95).

As a result of my sadness and fear, I spent most of my waking hours crying. Even in the midst of my grief and confusion, I found it astounding that the human body was capable of shedding so many tears! I cried, not only when I was alone, but also during any conversation I was forced to have with the outside world. I simply could not talk with anyone about anything without breaking into tears. Fortunately, I was later to learn that all this crying is biologically and psychologically healthy. According to Leick & Devidse-Nielsen:

> ...the great importance of weeping in grief work has
> become more and more evident...Weeping is important
> because in the tears there are forces that heal both
> physically and mentally (10).

In addition to the crying, I found myself sobbing heavily and involuntarily, even when I was not crying, as though my very soul were crying out in pain. This was an experience I had never had before, and I didn't really know what to make of it. The above authors had something to say about this as well:

> Weeping that heals [involves] profound sobbing in which,
> like a baby, [the griever] lets go of tensions [which] arise
> from the muscles of the body ... [acting] as a defense
> against both physical and mental pain (11).

Yet, it was my mind that was my most formidable nemesis during these agonizing months. I lived and relived my husband's death hundreds of times. I knew this type of thinking was futile and irrational, yet I continued to ask myself the same questions, over and over again: Could I have done anything differently? Would Jim have lived if we had not moved him to the cardiac hospital? Should I have insisted we take him to a hospital in San Francisco? How experienced were those doctors anyway? I knew enough about grieving and logical thinking to know that these questions were a waste of time, but my brain would not rest. It ruled, and I succumbed to its tyranny.

My only escape from this mental stress was sleep. I spent as much time as I could hiding under my blankets, seeking a semi-conscious state. Dreams were sometimes sweet, and I would awake comforted, thinking Jim was still alive, but when I was fully conscious, and discovered my dreams had deceived me, I was more miserable than ever. There were other times when I dreamed I spoke to Jim and begged him to let me be with him, but he would always say, "Jan, you know that isn't possible." So, though I sometimes escaped blissfully into my dreams, at other times the dreams became as heinous as reality itself.

Mornings were always bad. Jim and I had had a wonderful morning routine. In the spring, summer, and fall, we would sit on our lovely patio sipping coffee, reading the paper, and discussing our plans for the day. It was a delightful way to begin each new day, and both of us so much enjoyed that time together. Now, I spent my mornings drinking my coffee alone in the study. I could not bear to sit on the patio as Jim and I had done so often. It was simply too painful. Mitsch and Brookside, in *Grieving the Loss of Someone You Love*, understand so well the challenge of this time of day for the bereaved:

> Mornings take on a whole new meaning after the death of
> someone we love. We now dread what, once, we might

have greeted as the dawning of a day filled with
possibilities, new hopes, and the expected fulfillment of our
dreams. Now morning seems to slap us in the face with the
cruel reality of another day spent without the one we loved
so dearly (75).

If possible, evenings were even worse. Jim and I ended each day much
as we began it, on our patio surrounded by our garden. My husband would
mix us a cocktail and we would stroll through the yard inspecting his lat-
est acquisitions, he demonstrating their uniqueness, I admiring each and
every one of them. Then, we would share what the day had held for each
of us, as we sat watching the sun go down behind the tall oak trees that
flank our yard. Reflecting back on those evenings was the most difficult
time for me. It was by far the loneliest time of the day and caused me the
most suffering. Perhaps this is why it was during the night hours that
much of my behavior was so destructive. In short, I ate and drank. I have
heard that most women in my situation cease eating, causing the familiar
refrain from friends and relatives: "Dear, you must eat to keep up your
strength." Not I. Instead, I would often eat two and three meals in one
evening. I thought filling my stomach would stop its aching. But it didn't.
As a consequence, I gained forty pounds in four months. I didn't care. I
really didn't. As if that were not bad enough, I made it a practice of con-
suming a bottle of wine each evening. While the food had no positive
effect on my emotional state, the drinking did—it took the edge off my
pain. And it helped me sleep, along with the Valium tablet I consumed
each night before retiring.

In such a manner, my days passed, slowly and painfully. My thoughts
were constantly focused on Jim. I missed him terribly. Had no life without him. Only wanted to be with him. I wondered why Jim and I could not
have died together. A plane crash. An automobile accident. Whatever. Just
so the result was that I was with him. After all, we had spent most of our
adult lives together. In many ways we grew up together. Though the
expression has become trite, we truly were soul mates. Wasn't it quite natural, then, to contemplate the possibility of joining him? It seemed perfectly logical. I wanted to be with Jim. I was miserable without him. Why
not fix it?

To this end, I began creating a cache of prescription pills. There was, of
course, one very important impediment—the children. I knew my sons
could not endure the death of another parent at this juncture in their lives.
I realized that I was significant to them, not only because they loved me,
but also because I was the closest connection to their father, and therefore
necessary to their emotional healing. Consequently, I knew I would do

nothing impulsively, despite my fantasies. Yet, and this is important: It was a tremendous comfort for me to know that, if I could not bear the sorrow one more day, I did have, in my control, a way out.

It is imperative that I hasten to add that specialists in the field of grieving all agree that the above behavior is extremely dangerous. Mitsch and Brookside warn that professional help should be sought if you:

> Have Thoughts of suicide
> Find yourself using drugs (prescription or otherwise)
> Find yourself using alcohol in order to deal with your loss
> (35).

Therefore, be wise. If you find your behavior out of control in any way, or if you find your friends or relatives excessively concerned about you, turn to a professional for guidance. At this point in my grieving, I was a poster child for pathological behavior. Take my advice and use better judgment.

Jane's Sense of Self

Jane suffered from a sense of isolation as well. After many years of marriage, she lost her husband to a heart attack and suffered, not only grief, but a sense of her own identity:

I felt as though my husband's death diminished me. I lost the person who had been an integral part of my dreams, goals and memories. I felt smaller because of this loss, but also because of the realization of lost future experiences and charting my way through the large and small decisions still to come. My husband brought another perspective on the world, which enlarged my own. Whom would I now be able to depend on when I was making an important decision? Whom could I tell about seeing someone that looked just like that funny person we saw on our trip to the Grand Canyon? Or about something our oldest daughter did that reminded me of when she was three?

Jane's use of the word *diminished* to explain how she felt, now that she was a widow makes a lot of sense to me. As new widows, and for some time to come, we are unpracticed in making all the decisions by ourselves. We were used to consulting and sharing the responsibilities with our husbands. Sharing is a key word here, because it also relates to all those memories we have stored over the years. Reflecting on them with our partner was a pleasurable experience. Now that is gone forever.

Barbara's Pain

Barbara expressed similar emotions when she lost her husband, Bob:

I felt very much alone and this was a frightening experience for me...I cried, held his clothes, picked his hair off his chair, even asked my mother-in-law to move in with me (she declined). Sometimes during my grieving, I wondered if I was okay mentally. I spent my waking hours living in the past, picking out a special day I had spent with him and reliving it over and over.

Barbara couldn't tolerate the isolation any longer:

Finally, I decided I had to get out into the world and live the single life: I began dating several men, hoping to fill the void. I wanted my old life back with only one secure man in it, so I eventually married for a second time. Yet, to this day, I'd give the rest of my life to just sit in Bob's loving presence for ten minutes.

Barbara's story is similar to many women who must cope with enormous grief. They reach out for someone to fill that tremendous void in their soul. Many times this is successful. Foehners and Cozart believe that if a widow is inclined to date, she should take the plunge because:

> Long ago someone courted you, fell in love with you, and married you. Then, after years of being half a couple you became a single woman. Now even though your social life is full, you might enjoy a man inviting you out. For many women, it's nice to once again touch a rough tweed jacket, to smell after-shave or jut to share dinner with a man who doesn't belong to someone else! It would be a boost to feel desirable again, to know that someone would choose to spend time with you (182).

In other words, follow your instincts about how you deal with your new situation. Some of you will need more time than others. Some will be more comfortable returning to a social environment. Neither of these choices is more correct than the other. Your choice is the correct one!

7
Anger, Guilt, and Regret

During my time in isolation, I didn't realize that I was dealing with anger, along with all the other emotions that were plaguing me. I knew I was not angry with my husband for dying; after all, he was truly the victim in all this. And I really wasn't particularly angry with God either. Haven't we been told that the afterlife is better than this one? If so, wouldn't God consider taking Jim to a better place, a gift on His part? Anyway, I don't think I blamed God for this tragedy.

And yet, as I reflect back on my behavior, I realize that I was certainly angry with *someone*. Let me give you one example: In spite of our privacy management contract with the telephone company, my husband frequently received calls at night from salespeople. Before his death, I found these calls invasive, to be sure. Now I found them down right cruel, because they were reminders that Jim was no longer with me. Here is one example:

"Hello. Is Dr. Wright in?"

My caustic answer:

"Dr. Wright is dead."

Each call was like a stab in my heart, so I countered with rudeness. I actually gained a measure of perverse pleasure in doing so. I knew I was being offensive, but I didn't care.

Another situation that incurred my anger, which I now understand more clearly, came during the first Christmas holiday season after Jim's death. For the most part I received lovely messages from family and friends, sensitive to my new condition. However, one Christmas letter arrived from a woman I had not seen in years, but who was aware of Jim's death. It was full of good news and cheer, relating all the wonderful things she and her husband had done during the past year. I sat there in astonishment that an educated woman could be so insensitive as to send such a mailing to a grieving widow! I was not jealous of her happiness (God knows, I have learned we must grab such happiness when we can); but I did resent her detailing it to me at such a time in my life.

Now, as I reflect more rationally on my behavior during that time, I realize I *had* been angry and was either unwilling to admit it, or didn't recognize it as such. Foehner and Cozart in *The Widows Handbook* say anger is a normal part of the grieving process. Widows feel anger at the unfairness of their situation, and rightly so. Yet, these authors also warn the grieving widow that her wrath must be dealt with:

> If you had a dangerous hole on your front porch, you
> would not ignore it. You would resolve the problem by
> getting the hole repaired. The hole doesn't disappear by
> itself. Similarly, your anger doesn't go away by itself. You
> must not ignore or suppress your anger, but constructively
> express it (28).

Here are some suggestions they give as ways to deal with this pent-up anger:

> Express them to a therapist or a close friend.
> Cry or scream into a pillow.
> Shovel the snow or mow the grass.
> Join a widow's support group.
> Take a slow walk. Have a cup of tea.

I wish I had realized that I was angry during my time in isolation. Perhaps I could have focused on those emotions, brought them to the surface, and attempted to deal with them.

A Widow's Anger

During my grieving process, I spoke with a number of women who, even after many years of widowhood, are still angry with their husbands for dying. Having a partner becomes such an integral part of one's life, even when dealing with something as simple as getting help zipping one's dress or fastening a bracelet. Now these moments remind the widow that she can no longer depend on another to ease these frustrations.

It turns out that anger is a common emotion, which many widows endure. Leick and Davidsen-Nielsen put it this way:

> It takes a certain amount of courage to direct one's anger at
> the deceased...for the pain and meaninglessness that the
> grieving person feels.

The widow frequently suffers with thoughts such as:

How could you desert me, leaving me with thousands of
problems and responsibility....Why didn't you go to the
doctor five years ago when I told you to? Why didn't you
take more care of yourself so you didn't die? (48)

Guilt

My mother was widowed at the age of thirty-five. As if this were not
tragic enough, my father's death occurred in an auto accident, only hours
after they had argued, but had not had the opportunity to make up.
Because of this, my mother felt a good deal of guilt. I remember her
telling me more than once to never leave my spouse in a state of anger.
Her words rang true to me, especially since I knew they came from the
heart. But over the years of my own marriage, I came to realize that, no
matter how much two people love each other, they *will* have disagreements. It's part of the human condition. When I first married, my mother's
words haunted me if Jim ever left the house annoyed with me for one
thing or another (or I with him). Then, as I became more confident in the
soundness of our relationship and comfortable with our love for each
other, I realized that minor disagreements do not affect the core of a relationship. Spouses know they love each other, *even when they are angry*.

I was lucky. I was with Jim in his last hours. We had no unresolved
issues in our relationship and had been enjoying life to the fullest. But, if
my husband had died as my father had, I would still be comforted by the
knowledge that Jim knew I loved him dearly. I didn't need to be there to
say it. He knew. I wish my mother could have come to the same realization. It would have brought her some peace.

For those of you who were not with your husband when he died, or
were not on the absolute best of terms when the time came, please comfort yourself with the knowledge that your beloved knew of your love for
him. Couples don't live together for years without knowing these things,
even if they were left unspoken. If you are one of those widows who did
not have an opportunity to say everything you wanted to before your husband died, the above authors suggest this exercise:

> ...try writing a letter to your late husband. Tell him what
> you are feeling. Describe what you wish you had done or
> said.... Ask for his understanding...(31)

From my point of view, this is a wonderful way to speak to your
beloved. I believe most sincerely that he will know of your letter and be

moved by your writing it. No question, it will definitely ease your feelings of guilt that you do not deserve.

Yalanda's Feelings of Guilt

Though she knew that her feelings were ill founded, Yalanda suffered from guilt after the death of her husband. These are her words:

Tony had always been a healthy man, never sick. Then, one day he complained of not feeling well and spent hours that afternoon lying around the house. This was so rare, I became concerned and wanted to take him to the doctor, but Tony resisted, saying he would feel better in a day or so. Though I was somewhat concerned, I agreed to wait a little longer. But at dinner, my husband didn't feel well enough to eat and just wanted to go to bed. At this point I called my son and we took Tony to the hospital. It turned out he had pneumonia. He developed septicemia and died within twenty-four hours.

Yalanda, an experienced nurse, found it difficult to forgive herself for acquiescing to Tony's resistance to seeking medical help. But we all know how difficult it is to get someone (especially husbands) to see a physician if they do not wish to do so. Foehner and Cozart discuss this in *The Widows Handbook*:

> Guilt is defined as 'being responsible for an offense or wrongdoing.' In our grief, we may easily feel we are guilty or responsible for doing or not doing something that led to our husband's death. Guilt is the most difficult phase of Grief. It is sometimes felt as anger toward ourselves. It can be the most painful, the most self-destructive and the most difficult to resolve…. If you have unresolved anger or guilt, try writing a letter to your late husband. Tell him what you are feeling. Describe what you wish you had done or said. Write about your anger at yourself. Ask for his understanding, and try to forgive yourself (30/31).

Regret

Regret is another powerful emotion that often plagues widows. In truth, I do have some regrets. I don't give them leave to haunt me, but sometimes they do anyway. Even though my husband and I had forty-three years together, I regret that we did not have our retirement years to spend together. Family life is so busy; careers, children, and the like consumed us for many years. Not that we would have changed that for anything, it was probably the most meaningful thing we did. Still, those future years of togetherness in retirement were extremely appealing to contemplate. Jim was only retired ten months, which gave us a mere taste of what could have been. But I don't want to appear greedy. When I find myself in this mode of thinking, I remind myself that we had more years together than most couples, and they were good years.

Related to this is my regret that we didn't manage to visit Greece, a trip on which we were to embark in May, the month after Jim's death. This was a place that we both wanted to see, but Jim in particular. He had been reading about Greek history for months and knew more about that country than most people ever will. We also discussed Greek literature and architecture and were, to be sure, more than ready to begin that vacation. I have no interest in going to Greece without Jim, but I do regret that he didn't get to go. My regret, however, is tempered by the belief that he can now visit those magnificent isles in spirit!

One final regret is that I was not more of a financial partner during our marriage. I remember once when we were newlyweds Jim attempted to get me involved by having me take care of household expenses and record keeping. After one month, I told him I really didn't care for the job, since there didn't seem to be enough income to cover the expenses! I can look back on that young woman and smile at her foolishness. But in later years, I wish I had gotten involved in such matters, if only so that I could have communicated more knowledgeably with my husband about financial issues and been a better partner in this respect. If there is any consolation for me, it is that Jim enjoyed working with figures, both domestically and professionally. So I don't think he minded. Still, I wish I had taken more interest.

All the emotions mentioned above are a natural part of the grieving process. One can only recognize their presence and take action to deal with them. In subsequent chapters, I lay out a number of activities you can try which, hopefully, will aid you in finding relief. In the meantime, be assured that your emotions are normal. Accept them as their right to exist.

8
Harsh Realities

In spite of the emotional turmoil in my self-imposed isolation, it seemed preferable to what I encountered in the "real" world. At a time when I was physically and emotionally exhausted, I was inundated with important matters demanding my immediate attention: taxes, mortgage payments, insurance policies, medical bills, annuities—all the issues I had avoided during our marriage.

At this point, of course, I needed to know. And I needed to know, *now*. So, as the bills came in, I sat down, calmed myself, and called the respective companies. I explained that I was a neophyte at this entire business and requested their patience in explaining to me exactly what kind of policy or contract we had with them and what my responsibilities were. A piece of advice here: this is not a time in your life for false pride; you get much more accomplished by letting these people know you are a recent widow, haven't a clue as to what you are doing and need their help. By doing so, I found everyone was more than happy to be of assistance in any way they could, even willing to go the extra mile to give me additional good advice. It is not an exaggeration to say I was greatly depending on the kindness of strangers at this time, and things went more smoothly because of it.

With each call I made, I created a file in which I put copies of all papers I received from that company, all notes that I took when I talked with them regarding my responsibilities, and the name of a contact for future use. I entered reminders on my calendar concerning each payment I owed and when it was due. Furthermore, under advice, I put all contracts in my name. This was important, because, like it or not, I now had to establish my own credit rating. Believe me, none of this was easy to do. Every time I took my husband's name off a contract, I felt as though he were dying all over again.

Finances, then, were an ongoing problem. Remember my complaining about having to order death certificates at the funeral home? Well, now I discovered their importance! I needed proof of my husband's death at every institution I encountered. The first was our life insurance company. I found this contact particularly difficult because I didn't like the idea of receiving money for my husband's death. But, of course, such thinking was irrational. With no other income at the time, I was in need of those funds. All that was required of me was to give the company our policy number, and mail them a copy of the death certificate. In less than two weeks, I received a check, which was enough to keep me solvent until I could establish a regular income.

Still another important stop had to be made to my lawyer's office. My son, Joe, a law graduate, and I sat down with the lawyer and went over my husband's and my will, made a few changes in my new will, and discussed the execution of Jim's. Because I was the sole beneficiary of Jim's estate, the legalities were uncomplicated. Once again, I needed to give him a death certificate, which he submitted to the state with other official papers for probate. One suggestion: after a number of months have passed, you may want to take time to rethink your will now that your husband is deceased. Two years after Jim's death, I had my will rewritten with a number of significant changes that better suited my new situation. Because I was not thinking clearly, I could not have done that immediately after my husband's death.

Having completed the business with my lawyer, I turned my attention to resolving my Social Security benefits. (Here, also, you must take a death certificate.) I learned that if your husband earned a larger salary than you did, you are better off filing for social security as his widow, rather than in your own name. Ask them about this while you are there. If the representative is not helpful, call their 800 number. I must say, however, I found the social security people to be most obliging.

Closely related to social security benefits is health insurance, which a widow must deal with at this tumultuous time. Until this point in my life, I thought Medicare was all I required to cover any health problems I might develop. But, like everything else, it isn't that simple. I was informed I would be wise to take out a supplemental policy to cover what Medicare does not. After researching insurance policies and talking with a number of people, I discovered that no supplemental policy is ideal. Our policy to this point had been with an insurance company that my husband had joined through his university affiliation, and I elected to stay with them, at least for the time being. But I was disillusioned to learn that supplementary policies are quite expensive, especially if they cover a large part of your pharmaceutical needs, and add much to a widow's expenses.

Even more emotionally demanding for me was dealing with stocks and annuities. Though I was aware of the fact that we owned stocks, I had no idea in what companies or who was administering them. My sons retrieved the papers from my husband's files, and we began the process of determining what to do with these investments. Because Jim had our stocks invested through several companies, it seemed particularly confusing. One piece of information that hit home quickly was that before I even had time to focus on stocks, they had fallen considerably. (The nineties over, stocks had now turned south!) This I found frightening, since stocks and annuities would now be my only income. Thus, I reluctantly determined to make myself more astute about this confusing and chaotic world of finance, in hopes of gaining some control over my financial destiny.

The next stop to be made was to TIAA-CREF, the managers of my husband's annuity program, in which he had enrolled through the university. My son and my brother-in-law (who was also enrolled in TIAA-CREF) accompanied me to this important meeting. We needed to ascertain how much money had accrued in my husband's account and make some determination about how much I needed to draw out every month to meet my living expenses. This involved discussion about stocks, savings, portfolios, equities, principals, interest rates, investments, and so on. I might as well have been hearing all this in a foreign language! Eventually, however, we developed a plan to accommodate my needs, but I'm still working on understanding all this convoluted business and am determined to do so.

In spite of all the above transactions, my major concern still remained every day finances. Because I was so unsophisticated about our overall financial responsibilities, I continued to be terrified of the unknown. Every month I was hit with something I was not expecting. The most traumatic of my transactions involved the Indiana Revenue Department. Soon after my husband's death, I received a notice from this department that I owed them money for the previous year's taxes. Well, in my naiveté, I wrote them a very nice letter including a check for one-third the debt, telling them I would send them checks in the next two months to cover the entire amount of the debt. It seemed like the reasonable and responsible thing to do. It didn't, however, impress the tax people one iota! They slapped a fine on me and made it clear that if I needed more time to pay my taxes, I must come in and get official approval from them. One huge lesson learned: Don't mess with the Indiana Revenue Department!

Thus, my struggle with finances kept me in a state of anxiety—*high anxiety*. Because of this, the bank became my closest friend. I had not been inside a bank in ten years. Now I had to go in there at least the first of every month to withdraw cash and check on my account (always fearful I might overdraw). The cashiers provided me with a printout of the previous month's statement, so that I could begin to look at a whole month's activities at one time. In the end, I requested a printout of the entire last year's transactions, which made it possible for me to get an overall view of finances on a yearly basis. This way, I would no longer be blindsided every month by a bill I wasn't expecting. (In time I learned that most of my transactions, including ascertaining the state of my account, could be made over the Internet.) And so, slowly and painfully, I began to understand my finances. None of this happened dry-eyed. For six months, I cried through every transaction at the bank. When the clerks saw me coming through the door, they reached for their box of tissues!

Margaret Anne's Experience

Margaret Anne had an entirely different experience after her husband Gene died. Because his illness was a prolonged affair, there was ample time to discuss all the issues she would encounter after he died. They discussed what to do about the house and car (keep them), maintenance around the house (find a good handyman to help), and how to deal with finances (get a good financial advisor). Gene explained about their stocks and the money market and everything else he could think of that Margaret Anne needed to know. All this was painful at the time, but extremely helpful once she was a widow and forced to deal with all this herself.

Foehner and Cozart's *The Widows Handbook*, offers sound advice on finances and other matters facing widows. I wish I had discovered it sooner. It may well have saved me a good deal of anxiety. My recommendation is this: You are in no mental state to deal with financial problems after you lose your husband. Do as Margaret Anne did and find a *trusted* financial expert to help with the many issues that will be thrown your way during this most difficult of times. As time passes, you will be able to take more control, but don't trust yourself for the first year or two. If you have not been actively involved with these affairs, the learning curve is too steep to conquer in your present emotional state.

My Mother's Experience

Not every widow has the luxury of having finances available to her. Many widows, like my mother, *had* no finances. Like her, hundreds of widows are left with children to rear and no funds to fall back on. They have to worry constantly about keeping food on the table and roofs over their family's head. In my mother's case, she moved into government-subsidized housing, hired a sitter for her children, and went to work full time. There was never enough money, but she managed to keep her family together, though at great personal sacrifice. Such women, and there are legions, deserve our admiration, for they are the true heroines.

9
Reaching Out

Some time during the fourth month of my bereavement, I knew I needed to seek assistance in my struggle to deal with Jim's death. It was at this point, once again, I turned to books for guidance. What I learned in those books, I have been sharing with you in previous chapters and will continue to do so. A strong recommendation from many of the authors was "get counseling." They rightly pointed out that there are all kinds of possibilities out there for counseling.

One suggestion was to seek private therapy with a professional in psychiatry, psychology, or the ministry. Sitting and crying in front of a professional for an hour a week was not appealing to me. Perhaps I was not ready for the one-on-one attention (and pressure). Fortuitously, I learned that a local hospice center was forming a grief-counseling group to help those who had recently lost a loved one. Though I was not in any way enthusiastic about participating in such an activity, I intuitively knew that it was time I did something. In retrospect, it was a good decision, and one minor step toward recovery.

Our group was composed of twelve individuals, purposely kept small in order that there would be time for each person to be given adequate attention. We met once a week for three hours. The first evening we simply sat around in comfortable armchairs and introduced ourselves, explaining whom we had lost. "I'm Jan Wright. I lost my husband over four months ago to a massive heart attack." That was all there was to it—-and all I could have found the energy or courage to offer. The two leaders spent the rest of the time explaining how the group would function and what we would try to cover in our six-weeks of meetings. They made it clear to us that our participation was voluntary and that those of us who needed more time could listen to others who were ready to contribute. This most certainly put me at ease, as I really was not sure I wanted to be in the group in the first place, and I was definitely sure at this point that I did not want to participate.

In subsequent weeks, members of the group began to talk about their loved ones and how they had lost them. Some of those in the group had been in other grief-counseling situations, making them feel more at ease in this one. Eventually, however, everyone's story was told. Listening to these sad people was a heart-wrenching experience. But it was obvious that telling their stories and expressing their sorrows provided each person with a profound sense of relief. In fact, the counselors explained to us that if the survivor does not find some way to open her heart to others, she is in danger of remaining closed for the rest of her life.

Another important point to be made here: as a grieving listener, I came to the surprising realization that I could grieve for another person in pain! Until now, I only cared about my own suffering. I am now convinced that the ability to truly *feel* compassion for another person's pain is a significant step toward healing. Grieving for oneself, no matter how justified and understandable, is an egocentric activity. It is necessary, of course, but it is not enough.

The Dalai Lama puts it this way: "All the world's major religions stress the importance of cultivating love and compassion." This empathy, [i.e.] our ability to share others' suffering, he teaches, "has universal implications" for all of us. I firmly believe this is so, for I have experienced first hand a deeper sense of empathy for others since I myself have suffered such pain. As the Dalai Lama explains, this compassion for others "puts us in fundamental oneness" with the rest of our human family (123). Indeed, do we not all suffer at some time in our lives? Would we not all be better off if we could show more compassion to others when they are in pain?

In each session the leaders focused on particular problems facing members of the group. And there were many: family squabbles over inheritance, other financial difficulties, sleeping and eating disorders, loneliness, and so on. Sometimes merely describing the problem was enough, but there were people with various backgrounds in the group who could offer excellent advice for those who were troubled. For example, a lawyer advised a member of the group on her problems with estate settlement.

Interestingly enough, even though I had been told privately by one of the counselors that suicide and sex were weighty problems for survivors, neither the leaders nor the group members brought up these subjects. So, weeks after we began our meetings, when I was feeling more at ease, I brought up the subject of suicide. I admitted that I had had such thoughts, thus encouraging another member to admit the same. Yet, I was surprised that no one else spoke of such inclinations, especially given the intensity of sorrow that permeated the group. In the end, I regretted that I had brought up the subject, as I was contacted the next day by the person in charge of the counselors who questioned me about my intentions in this matter. Only by assuring him that I was not in any imminent danger, did he feel comfortable enough to let me off the hook. When I complained that

I was told our group sessions were confidential, he exclaimed, "In every-thing except suicide."

The other issue mentioned above, which I did not bring up, especially after my debacle concerning suicide, was sex. If the counselors believed it to be an important issue with surviving spouses, why didn't they bring it up? Perhaps, because the group was of mixed-gender, it seemed too awkward. But then most of what we discussed was to some extent awkward. Judy Tatelbaum's comments on this subject are helpful:

> Sexuality is deeply affected by grief. After the loss of a spouse, sexual frustration may be an intense source of anguish. But there is also a natural emotional withdrawal during mourning that may cause a diminishing or a total loss of interest in sex. Sometimes the pleasure of intimacy may produce guilt or anxiety during the initial weeks of mourning, or we may find our sexual needs intensified. Confusion reigns when we are torn between the need and wish for closeness, on the one hand, and detachment and lack of sexual responsiveness on the other. Masturbation may help diminish sexual tension and frustration (32).

She goes on to say:

> Sexual dysfunctions of various kinds, such as impotence and premature ejaculation in men, and inability to respond to attain orgasm in women, occur during the early months of bereavement. [However], Symptoms ... of sexuality usually subside with understanding, tolerance, and patience (32-3).

If our counselors did not feel comfortable bringing up this subject with the group, perhaps they could have given us a handout on this matter. At this time in my life, sexuality was not an issue for me, but I have since discovered that it is for many others.

In the final weeks of the group, members were encouraged to bring in special mementos of their lost loved ones. This was an extremely moving experience for everyone. Most brought in photographs and other items that were especially relevant. As these were passed around, the survivor shared memories that were of special meaning. I did not believe that I would be able to perform this task and did not do so until the very last minute. When I did, I showed the group a drawing Jim had made (only months before his death) of our house, for one of our son's birthday. I also showed them a picture of him as a curly-haired child and another of him as an adult. During this time, I played for them a tape I had of Jim's piano playing. Though the experience was difficult, when it was over, I was glad that I had made the effort. I felt as though I had, in some small manner, given honor to my husband.

The group's final meeting was extremely moving. We all sat around a table with unlighted candles in front of us. The first member's candle was lit, and she was directed to express what her lost love had given her in their lifetime together. When finished, she lit the candle of the member seated next to her, and the ritual continued. When it was my turn, I said: "I light this candle for my husband, Jim, whom I loved dearly, and who gave me his love and support for forty-three years. He taught me to appreciate the beauty of all living things from the most magnificent of nature's creations to its smallest insect. I request all of you to remember us in your prayers, and I will remember all of you in mine."

By the time all the candles were lit, there was not a dry eye in the room. But we all knew we had participated in a meaningful ritual, one that honored our loved ones, and one that honored each person in the room.

Then it was over. All hugged, extended well wishes, and promised to stay in touch. Some would join subsequent groups. I knew I would do neither. For me the experience and the group existed in a certain, special time and space. I had no intention of tampering with that experience.

In this manner, I took a step toward recovery. To this day, I am grateful that I found the courage to do so. And it did, indeed, take courage. I had to force myself to go to that first meeting. I chose a group situation because I didn't want the pressure of a one-on-one situation, but you may be more comfortable meeting alone with a counselor.

Interestingly enough, many of the widows I spoke with, no matter what their religious affiliation, turned to their churches for emotional and spiritual support after their husbands died. Some joined counseling sessions; others became involved with prayer or bible study groups. Some joined the church choir. Whatever their choices and whatever their religion, the women found a source of community and solace. It doesn't matter what you choose, but do make yourself reach out. I promise you will be happy you made that decision. Good luck!

10
Baby Steps

The group counseling was over, and I once again returned to a state of isolation, but with a difference. Many of us in the group had not ventured from our homes in weeks or months except to attend those meetings. We were not willing to expose ourselves to society and what it might demand of us. The counselors, however, were there with some suggestions, which I thought were exceptionally creative. One in particular they called "baby steps." Group participants, for the most part, were under the illusion that venturing out into society meant full steam ahead, all or nothing. But the counselors made it clear that we could indulge in baby steps instead. For some this meant simply walking around their yards, then down the street, and finally, through the neighborhood. Baby steps, yes, but steps, just the same. Some in the group were more assiduous. One young woman stated that she was invited to a dance with a girlfriend but was afraid to go. It was suggested by the counselors that she attend the dance, but agree to stay only thirty or forty minutes. The thinking being that she would have the courage to go if she knew she would not be locked into a prolonged evening that might cause her undue stress. The woman went to the dance, took the counselor's advice, and succeeded. Baby steps had worked. This struck me as a wonderful solution to moving back into society and still protecting myself. I made a mental note to use this when the occasion arose.

Another suggestion was to plan a coffee date with a trusted friend. Not a luncheon, as that might be too stressful. If coffee went well, it might be extended to include lunch, but the bereaved would not be committed. Meeting a friend for a movie is another possibility, because there is no pressure to carry on a conversation. For the athletically inclined, a morning run with an acquaintance (or alone) might be a good idea. Attending a religious service is another means of beginning one's "safe" entrance back into society. Of course, not all widows suffer from social phobia during this time in their lives. But for those who do, it is helpful to have some creative ideas for dealing with the problem. It is comforting also to realize this feeling will pass, and it will become easier and easier to socialize, but the first few occasions might be difficult. So take baby steps.

I took my baby steps solo. My husband and I had joined a health club near our home. I was not yet prepared to rejoin my aerobics group, but I did miss another facet of our club—the pool. Water has always been a source of comfort to me (my husband often said I was surely a dolphin in my last life). Consequently, I began going to the club during off-hours, (diner time, etc.) when I knew I would be assured privacy. It got me out of the house and afforded me an opportunity to exercise my body and soothe my soul without having to endure the solicitations of members.

Later, when I thought I was ready, I carefully chose my first social outing—I had a quiet dinner out with a close friend. It was not a particularly courageous choice, as I had dined with her many times before, but it seemed bold now. It was, after all, my first social outing as a widow and I was not sure how I would feel. Somehow, going out with my female friends as a married woman had always seemed safe to me (I never feared that I would be suspected of being "on the hunt" for a male companion). Would I feel differently now? But the evening went smoothly. Truth be told, I'm old enough at this point that the problem of encountering men interested in pursing me is slim (if not downright non-existent!) And that's the way I want it. I worked hard on my relationship with my husband, and it was extremely rewarding, but I do not believe, at this point of my life, I am meant to focus my energy on another intimate relationship. I have too many other facets of my life on which I must concentrate.

One related point to make here: It has been discussed in a number of books I have read and in several conversations I have had with other widows, whether or not a widow should continue to wear her wedding ring. People come down on both sides of this question, but I consider this a decision that should be made by the widow herself, not society. I plan to continue to wear my rings, but I truly believe this is a personal choice. Some widows, and especially younger widows, at some point may very well wish to consider the possibility of remarriage. Therefore, each widow should decide for herself. Incidentally, her choice, in no way, reflects on her feelings for her late husband! Many women who dearly loved their husbands choose to keep their wedding rings in a safe place, where they remain a cherished symbol.

My next "baby step"—which did not seem like a baby step to me—was returning to my regular aerobics class. This was different than dinner out with a friend because it meant subjecting myself to a number of people, all at one time. I had been attending this class for several years before this tragedy, and was friendly with everyone in the class. When Jim died, I had sent word that when I returned I didn't want to talk about him or the circumstances surrounding his death. That, I knew, would be more than I could bear. I let them know that a hug from everyone would be nice, but nothing more. When the day came, it was all I could do to walk into that room. It was fortunate that I had prepared them and myself for this moment, because all of us were more comfortable knowing how to manage such an awkward encounter.

Thus, I measured out my recovery in baby steps. Some were relatively easy to take. Others were more difficult and took more courage. For those who have not gone through the grieving process, using words like "courage" to speak of such encounters sounds hyperbolic, but widows understand precisely what I mean. Each social action at this point in the recovery process calls for every ounce of grit. But it is crucial that the effort be made. And if it fails the first time, try again. It will pay off in dividends, and it really does get easier. Not right away, but in time. I promise.

In the meantime, there are so many little things you can do to ease your pain and anxiety. Here are a few examples:

> Soak in a hot tub with only candles illuminating the room.
> Walk barefoot in the grass.
> Get a massage.
> Look at the sky on a starry night.
> Say a prayer.
> Light a scented candle.
> Fill a vase with your favorite flowers.
> Watch a good video.
> Visit a place of worship when no one is there and sit quietly.
> Read an entertaining novel.
> Talk to your inner child and assure her you are there for her.

As you can see, the list focuses on pampering your body and soul. Use your imagination, and come up with ideas of your own. You deserve it.

11
Spiritual Steps

Moving cautiously back into society was a positive step toward healing, to be sure. But it was only part of what needed to happen in my life. I was all too aware that my mind, body, and spirit were connected, or should be, and much was lacking in this regard. In *Soul Print* Marc Gafni, a Jewish scholar, made a significant impression on me when he wrote:

> How does one reach the inside of God?
> Through reaching the inside of yourself.
> If you can stand inside yourself, then you are inside of God (262).

I knew that, in contrast to going back into society, this would require going inside *myself*. But how could I do that? It wasn't possible to escape to a monastery where I could avoid all distractions and just think.

Nature

I turned instead to my garden, where I could put myself in touch with nature, and hopefully gain some insights into my spiritual needs. It was fall and much needed to be done in the garden anyway, so I threw myself into outdoor projects. Transplanting shrubs gave me the opportunity to get my hands down in the soil, to move the earth, to communicate with the worms, apologizing for disturbing their universe, and asking their help in providing a favorable environment for their new neighbors. I was entertained by the squirrels scurrying around the yard, absorbed in burying their acorns for a winter harvest. I listened to the medley of birds singing and busying themselves at the feeders nearby. The autumn sun warmed my face, butterflies fluttered around the late-blooming flowers, and chipmunks scampered across the patio. I was so grateful to be even a small participant in this wonderful world of nature! It was my opportunity to just *be in the moment* and absorb the extraordinary atmosphere around me. All this lent itself well to what I needed. I highly recommend communing with nature to anyone looking for an opportunity to escape the chaos of life and concentrate on the condition of one's spirit.

Meditation

I discovered that my garden was also a perfect place to work on my meditative skills, which were primitive, to say the least. Many years before, I had read some instructions on how to go about meditating, so I decided to try them. The first one merely suggested that I sit quietly and comfortably in a calm environment, and begin to concentrate on my breathing. Continuing the concentration, I was to chase away any thoughts that came into my mind, and return to the breathing. This is a very simple form of meditation, but it does provide a calming influence and, after enough practice, promises to help you gain insight into your own spirit. I like this form of meditation because it is relatively easy, especially for a novice.

Another meditative practice I tried involved, again, sitting comfortably and concentrating on my breathing. Once this was accomplished, I was to envision myself as a tree rooted firmly in the ground. The meditation continuing, I (the tree) was required to pull free of my earthly moorings and rise slowly into the sky. As I rose higher and higher, I was to look down on the world and watch it fade away, leaving me emotionally unbound from my worldly cares.

Still another practice suggested in my readings also requires the use of imagination. After the initial requisite breathing exercise, I envisioned that I was in an elevator which was descending deeper and deeper into the ground until the elevator and I reached the earth's center, or core. This is an easy exercise to perform, and I found the sensations accompanying it quite inspiring.

All these practices have the same goal: to distract the meditator's mind from everyday concerns and free it to experience new spiritual dimensions. These meditative practices have been helpful to me as are others I have tried. However, when I am feeling lazy (which is more often than not) I take the easy path and turn to Dr. Andrew Weil's compact disk on meditation. In his soft, reassuring voice, he takes the listener through eight wonderful meditations that carry the mind far out into the awesome, vast universe and then back to earth and into the very blood vessels of one's own body. I find this experience extremely rewarding and recommend it highly. Meditation is an ancient practice that has become popular today to aid the voyager in uniting the mind, body and spirit. Give it a try. I think you will be pleasantly surprised with the results!

Music

Music, like nature and meditation, soothes the soul. It is said to be the universal language, and it is true that music can touch our hearts and souls no matter what language we speak. I prefer classical music, but my son, Steve, has introduced me to many other genres, including jazz, blues, and folk. Recently I was introduced to Enya's ethereal voice and purchased "A Day Without Rain." I also very much enjoy Josh Groban for his lovely voice and soothing lyrics. Finally, at night, just before climbing into bed, I put on "Sound Body, Sound Mind, Music for Healing" by Dr. Andrew Weil, who has designed this compact disk for relaxation and healing. As you know, there are countless tapes and CD's on the market; so take time to visit your local music store and listen to a number of them. You will find many to your liking, and you will experience joy in the listening.

The Experts

Still, I knew there was more I could do to heal my spirit and help me evolve into a stronger person. I prayed, of course, every day, but that was not enough. I needed assistance. So, back to the bookstore. Sure enough, the shelves were brimming with advice on improving the body, mind and spirit. I wanted to investigate a variety of approaches on the subject, so I could get a spectrum of ideas, even though I knew I would eventually narrow in on several favorites for my own use. Again, I like to own my books, because frequently I return, time and time again, to my favorites to reread parts of them, as reminders of important points that I may have forgotten.

One book I enjoy rereading is the sweet, gentle writing of a Vietnamese Buddhist monk named Thich Nhat Hanh titled *The Miracle of Mindfulness*, which is an easy read on meditative practice. His writing has a quality of simple goodness about it that brings peace to my soul. Here is one example:

> Every day we are engaged in a miracle which we don't
> even recognize: a blue sky, white clouds, green leaves, the
> black, curious eyes of a child—our own two eyes. All is a
> miracle (12).

Hanh knows that most of us go through life with our minds somewhere in our past or our future, rarely in the moment we are living. The art of mindfulness means to live in the moment, to focus on what we are doing *right now*. If you are relating to someone, for example, focus all your energy on that person and *really hear* what he or she is saying. I have put this into practice and discovered the other person is extremely grateful for the undivided attention. It is a small gift to give another human being!

And this does not just apply to people. Hanh also reminds us that: when we do household work such as washing dishes, dusting and wiping off tables, scrubbing the kitchen floor, arranging books on their shelves, whatever the tasks, do them slowly and with ease, *in mindfulness*. Don't do any task in order to get it over with. Resolve to do each job in a relaxed way, with all your attention. Enjoy and be one with your work (28/9).

How often when we are washing dishes do we actually *look* at those dishes, admire their beauty and think about where we purchased them, or perhaps they were a wedding gift, and how much we loved this new acquisition at the time. We all have many lovely things in our house that we were attracted to because of their beauty. How often do we really *look* at them with a sense of appreciation? My mother used to say "A thing of beauty is a joy forever." You get the idea.

Soul Prints is also a spiritual guide with which I have been quite impressed. Marc Gafni offers a practical and insightful book for anyone interested in pursuing a more authentic way of life. His theory is that we each have our own soul identity, our "soul print," and his goal is to help us uncover that identity and aid us in strengthening it. In the beginning of his book, Gafni gives practical suggestions on how the reader can become reacquainted with her own soul. For example, in one activity, the reader is shown how to make her own metaphorical "soul print box," in which she puts her "authentic stuff," the things that "really matter to her." Later in the book, once the reader has a better understanding of who she is, she begins the work of understanding and improving her soul print. Here is one "soul print practice" Gafni offers:

> In C. S. Lewis's children's novel *The Lion, the Witch, And the Wardrobe*, the Wardrobe is the symbol of the access point that we need to open in order to begin the journey. We need to find the right words, touch the right place in the wall, or have both halves of the ring in order for "Open sesame" to work. This first step is essential to the journey. First steps require a combination of magic and courage. Think of one area in which you want to make a breakthrough. Now, list five first steps that you could take to set the game in motion (290).

Through Gafni's guidance, the reader slowly begins to gain insight into her own mind and spirit and acquires ways to enhance both. Learning about oneself in this way is an enjoyable experience and remarkably enlightening. After all, if we do not know ourselves, how can we possibly know others?

Jack Kornfield's *A Path with Heart* is yet another excellent guide for the spiritual voyager. In this book, the author focuses a good deal of time on healing the body, the mind, and the spirit. He sees each as an important part of the whole and discusses ways to aid the reader in developing a healthy, "unified system." In one exercise, that I found distinctly relevant, the reader is shown how to transform sorrow into compassion. Another I especially like is a meditation on "Who Am I?" But perhaps my favorite exercise is the following:

> Picture or imagine that this earth is filled with Buddhas,
> that every single being you encounter [today] is
> enlightened, except one—yourself! Imagine that they are
> all here to teach you. Whoever you encounter is acting as
> they do solely for your benefit, to provide just the teachings
> and difficulties you need in order to awaken [learn]. Sense
> what lessons they offer to you…. Throughout the day
> continue to develop the image of enlightened teachers all
> around you. Notice how it changes your whole perspective
> on life (82).

If this sounds nonsensical to you, let me explain how I have come to see it: If I am standing in a long line at the grocery store and must wait while a rather slow, poorly trained, sales person clumsily attempts to run the cash register, I have a choice: lose my temper, and make my impatience known, or wait patiently. The more frequently I choose to practice patience and self-control, the better I get at it and, hopefully, the better person I become. In this way, Kornfield would suggest the "Buddha" cashier is aiding me in my spiritual growth.

In another of Thich Nhat Hanh's book *Being Peace*, he also deals with this subject: "*In the case of a minor irritation, the recognition of the presence of the irritation, along with a smile and a few breaths, will usually be enough to transform the irritation into something more positive, like forgiveness, understanding and love. Irritation is a destructive energy. We cannot destroy the energy, we can only convert it into a more constructive energy*" (41).

One final point on spiritual practices: I culled from Deepak Chopra's book *The Seven Spiritual Laws of Success* the following list of suggestions to enhance one's spirituality. I typed up the concepts and keep them on my refrigerator to remind me of practices I really want to follow on my spiritual journey:

1. I will take time each day to just be silent and listen to the universe.
2. I will spend some time in nature every day, which I hope will give me access to infinite creativity, freedom, and bliss.
3. Whenever I go into the chaos of the world, I will carry stillness within me.
4. I will practice non-judgment.
5. Wherever I go I will give whomever I meet a gift. This will be gift of a smile, a compliment or even a silent thought of good will.
6. I will accept graciously any gift that is offered to me.
7. I will remind myself everyday that my actions have consequences and that it is important to consider those consequences before taking action.
8. I will not only listen to my head (which might not lead me in the correct direction) but to my heart, which could very likely be closer to my spirit and therefore to the truth.
9. I will expend no energy trying to persuade others of my point of view. I will respect their point of view even though they do not respect mine. They have a right to theirs; I have a right to mine. My energy is better spent on positive matters.
10. I will remind myself of intellectual humility.
11. I will practice mindfulness. When I am dusting, I will be mindful of this task. I will appreciate the beauty of the furniture I am dusting, of the beauty of the tree from which the furniture came, etc. I will resist thinking of something I would rather be doing.
12. I will accept the fact that I am not in control of my environment, I will allow others the freedom to be as they are and not impose on them my idea of how things should be.

Above are only a few examples of the many, many books available on ways to search for more insight into who you really are—your authentic self. What I like about such approaches is that they not only lead me into my heart and soul, making me a better person, but send me back into the world, hopefully, a more insightful, kinder person, one who will be more understanding of my fellow human beings. All of this, of course, you will want to do in small steps. Begin with a few individuals and move out from there. I believe, most sincerely, you will find it rewarding.

Yet, even as you do so, please do not forget to continue your forays into nature and meditation, which will strengthen your resolve as you move forward in your search for self-discovery.

12
Possibilities

It has been six years now since I lost my husband. There is no question that I have come quite a long way. I have been working on spiritual steps, but more work needs to be done on the pragmatic side. If Jim had lived, I would have been content to focus my love and energy on him and the activities we would have pursued together. But since that is not to be, I must consider other possibilities—think about what I want to do with the rest of my life. When I first began contemplating possibilities, I anticipated the task to be an easy one. After all, the community offers uncountable opportunities to become involved. All I needed to do was choose. But, as I began to think about the options, I realized that I wasn't starting in the right place. How can I choose where to expend my energies before I take an in-depth look at who I am at this point in my life and seriously consider in which direction I wish to move? After all, I don't want to make frivolous choices and waste these precious years; I want to choose activities that will help me evolve into the person I am destined to be. I do not wish to merely pass the time still left to me in some impulsive manner. With these thoughts running through my head, the task of deciding what to do with the rest of my life seemed more daunting. So, once again I turned to the experts for guidance.

Similar themes flowed through all the books I read. One important point made by the experts is that when someone is faced with the necessity for change, she becomes fearful. It is true that most of us widows have formerly been in a safe place. Our lives were ordered and pleasant. But like it or not, we are faced with the fact that we must now make some changes, not because we want to, but because we have to. I am convinced that no widow should make major changes in the first year or so after her husband's death. We just aren't thinking clearly enough for added upheaval of any kind. But the time comes when changes must be made. In *The Power of Resilience*, Brooks and Goldstein understand the difficulty of this challenge but urge the reader to move forward:

> Unfortunately, some people would rather remain in a
> familiar situation associated with stress, isolation, and

> unhappiness than venture forth into unknown territory they fear may be even more dangerous. We must all learn to appreciate the benefits of change even as we recognize the possible dangers (171).

In the above quote, the word *danger* is referring to the psychological side of our selves. If we take steps toward change, will we fail? Will our family and friends accept us? Will we be criticized? Risk is always involved in change, but when the time comes, it is important for our development that we move in that direction. This move may be in the form of tiny steps, as we discussed earlier. Fine. Small steps are quite acceptable. No one will expect us to take up skydiving!

Another important theme in my reading related to the needs of our unconscious selves. Most writers seem to believe that in order to make decisions about our future and the changes we want to make, we must listen to our inner voice. We all have one, as you have seen in earlier chapters. But if we tend to be busy all the time, distracted by all the noise around us, we may not have taken the opportunity to be quiet and just let our inner self come to the forefront of our consciousness.

Perhaps my favorite book dealing with this is *Soul Mapping* by Frost, Ruge, and Shoup. They believe to make changes in your life, you need to start by taking a good look at who you are *today*. (Their theory being that you need to know who you are at this moment before you consider changes for the future.) A list of questions is presented to aid the reader in gaining insight into her present life, such as her relationships with friends, her activities, her worries, her fears, her joys, and so on. Answered honestly, the reader can begin to map out who she is at this moment, making it possible to take the next step.

This accomplished, a woman needs to examine important aspects of her past. What "tapes" have been running through your head from childhood? How were you perceived by your parents? Your siblings? Your friends? Your educators? How did you perceive yourself? How have these perceptions affected your life? The answers to these questions could have a tremendous effect on what decisions you make for your future. For example, if significant adults in your past encouraged you to take risks, to believe you could succeed in your endeavors, you are much more likely to face the future with confidence, than if you grew up with the belief that you were somehow lacking. If you have negative tapes playing in your head, it is wise to acknowledge their presence. Then, dismiss them. In their place, position new concepts, which focus on your abilities and accomplishments. Remember, your mind can be your enemy or your friend. When it tries to send you negative messages, messages that are not true or are no longer true, reject them and force your mind to focus on positive messages.

I picked up an informative little book entitled *You can Be happy No Matter What* by Richard Carlson, Ph.D., who spends considerable time warning his readers that our thoughts can be our nemesis; consequently, we must beware of the amount of stock we place in them:

> Your thought system contains all the information you have
> accumulated over your lifetime. It is [this] past information
> that your thought system uses to interpret the relative
> significance of everything that happens in your life
> [today]....Because our thought systems are filled with our
> memory of the past, information we have accumulated
> throughout our lifetimes, they encourage us to continue to
> see things in the same way. We react negatively (or
> positively) to the same situations or circumstances over and
> over again, interpreting our current experiences in life as
> we have in the past (20-1).

It is wise, therefore, to be the master of your thought system and insist that it work *for* you, not *against* you.

Ridding yourself of negative messages frees you to investigate other areas of yourself. Frost and company encourage the reader to explore childhood fantasies. We all had them, and they still reside in our unconscious, which means they are still a significant part of us. Exploring these fantasies might give some insight into your authentic self and into possibilities for the future. For example: As a little girl I loved to fantasize that one day I would be on stage and perform a remarkable tap dance routine in front of all who knew me, (but had no idea how talented I was). Well, I am never going to be on stage, and I never learned to tap dance, but I do love to dance and always have. I recognize and accept this as part of my authentic self and have joined a Zumba dance class at my health club to satisfy that part of my nature. Thus, I have brought dance back into my life with the added benefit of an aerobic workout!

Volunteerism

There are so many opportunities for widows to get involved in the community and be of tremendous help to others. Some of the widows I spoke with volunteer in nursing homes, others tutor children, and many give their time in offices where more hands are needed. I have talked with widows who work in hospitals delivering mail and flowers to patients. Others work in orphanages playing with the children. Several women, after their husbands died, went to work in hospices having had first-hand experience of the wonderful assistance they had been given during their difficult time. The opportunities for helping the community are endless. Check with your friends, look in the newspaper for suggestions how you can be helpful. Widows find volunteering some of their time to others makes them feel significant and gives them much joy. The Dalai Lama has written that our greatest joy "comes when we are motivated by concern for others" (62). All of us have experienced this in our lives at one time or another and know it to be true.

Hobbies

Our hobbies are another clue to our authentic self. All of us were involved in activities that we enjoyed over the years, or wish we had become involved with, but never did. This is a good time to review those areas, which have attracted our attention in the past. It is an opportunity to get reacquainted with the activity and with others who are interested in the same pleasures. Bridge clubs are popular in many communities, and most offer brush-up courses for those who have not played in awhile. This activity is entertaining and offers opportunities for making new acquaintances that share one of your interests. In addition, playing bridge is an excellent way to keep your mind active and young.

I rather backed into my hobby. My husband and I had long been interested in ancestry and had done some research on our families. (My mother once warned me that I would probably find most of our Irish relatives in pubs!) Anyway, one day it occurred to me that I should organize our files and make family albums for my sons and grandchildren.

This endeavor has been both a challenge and a joy. When I'm surrounded by all the pictures and documents, I find my mind transported back in time and relive so many interesting experiences that my family and my husband's family lived. Stories of hardships and successes abound, and I find myself feeling as though I am part of their stories. Not only do I have the joy of this process, but I have the added satisfaction of knowing I am passing all this on to my descendants!

Travel

Travel should also be considered if you enjoy visiting new places. As a teenager, I dreamed of faraway lands and, even though my husband and I traveled extensively, I still get the urge to take a trip from time to time. In most cases, however, widows do not want to travel alone and may have difficulty finding someone to travel with them. Consequently, it is important to know that there are many opportunities for those who have no one with whom to travel. Most communities offer a number of avenues for a single woman to travel safely and satisfactorily. Various local organizations, which are populated with other single people who love to travel, offer trips throughout the year. In addition, Elderhostel, a nation-wide organization offers many trips each year within the United States and abroad. All of these organizations assume the responsibility of making the necessary arrangements and leave you free to enjoy yourself. You will be surprised how many people take advantage of such opportunities. I have traveled alone on several occasions and can assure you, you will find many friendly travelers who will include you in their plans. In reality, you are more likely to meet new and interesting people if you are traveling alone, than if you are with another person. Take the risk. It's worth it!

But I do not want to discourage you from seeking out women, like us, who are searching for someone with whom to travel or simply with whom to socialize. Since I have become a widow, I have discovered that there are countless women who are also alone. Many of them would be delighted to form compatible friendships. Because they have been through similar tragedies, they are particularly excellent companions. So, keep your eyes open for the chance to develop such acquaintances.

Continuing Education

I do want to mention one more opportunity: Education. It comes in so many forms these days that you have numerous attractive choices. Senior organizations have mini courses in everything from flower arrangement to estate planning. Churches offer classes on matters of ethics and religion. Book clubs abound with opportunities to meet new people and discuss books of interest. Museums offer art appreciation workshops. And your local colleges have adult courses in every imaginable subject. My brother-in-law, a physician, is still taking courses at the age of seventy-eight! He loves the intellectual stimulation and the opportunity to delve into areas outside his profession. Have no fear that you will not be up to the challenge. Mark Twain once said that education was wasted on the young. Many professors obviously agree, confessing that they enjoy their older students more than the younger ones because of the experience and interest they bring with them to the classroom.

So, the possibilities are, indeed, endless. The question is: What is right for you? The statement that this is the first day of the rest of your life is trite but true. Make up your mind that you will not spend your widowhood shut off from the world. Begin to reflect on who you were, who you are, and who you still want to become. You are the artist as well as the object d'art. Make it your best work yet. Make it a masterpiece!

Afterword

When I began this book, I believed that grief and recovery were separate, and that one would follow the other. But I discovered that this is not so. Almost from the beginning, while in a state of terrible grief, healing is beginning, slowly but surely. We cried because we were sad, and at the time it would have been impossible for us to believe that this crying was actually helpful. Yet, it was, for that crying released emotions that had been fiercely building inside us. I also learned that reasonable isolation from the community is part of the healing process, for it provides a kind of "holding place" where we were free to reflect on what we have lost and begin to come to terms with what this would mean for us.

If anyone had told me in those dark, early days that I was actually beginning to heal, I would have thought that person delusional. But it is crucial for the widow to grasp this important concept at some level of her being i.e. the assurance of continued healing, because it provides the much-needed promise for her future well being. The promise is valid. The proof will come with time.

Am I promising you a rose garden? No. They only exist in fairy tales. After six years, I still miss my husband immensely. I still cry when I think of him, but not with the intensity or frequency that I did in my early grieving period. Perhaps it is possible that one is never completely free of grief for one loved so much. And that's okay. Jim was the most important person in my life. I learned much from him, and what I learned will continue to influence me for the rest of my life. Indeed, I like to think he, in some way, is still with me on my journey and when it is over, we will meet again. In the meantime, I have the rest of my life to live and I'm going to get on with it. Hopefully, you will do the same.

As I wrote this book, I could not help but think of myself as part of a community of widows, as though we are joined together in some kind of unique spiritual consciousness. I hope, as you took this journey with me, you had some of the same feelings. I further most sincerely hope that you will gain the strength to move forward with your life and make it all it can be. God Speed.

About The Author

Janet Wright was born in Cincinnati, Ohio the first of three daughters. Due to the tragic death of her father, she grew up in a household of all women, an experience in interesting juxtaposition to the one she would later have as the only female in a house of five males. In Cincinnati, Ms. Wright (then Ms. Bayer) began her higher education at the University of Cincinnati, studying business administration, which she later changed to a major in English Literature. Janet remained in Cincinnati until she married Dr. James J. Wright of Indiana. The couple spent the first two years of their marriage in Saigon, Vietnam, where Dr. Wright served in the army as Medical Director of the United States Dispensary. Ms. Wright became assistant to the director of Pan American World Airlines for Southeast Asia. While in this position, she and her husband had the opportunity to travel around the world and experience many fascinating cultures. They also fostered a war orphan, who is now residing in Missouri, the proud mother of two children of her own.

Upon returning to the states, Dr. Wright became Medical Director of the Community Mental Health Center in Indianapolis, Indiana. For the next seventeen years, Janet oversaw the upbringing of the couple's four sons, finished her graduate work in English Literature, did volunteer work tutoring in local schools and held positions of leadership in parent organizations. Eager to put into practice all she had learned about academia, Ms. Wright accepted a position teaching English literature to upper school students at Park Tudor Preparatory School in Indianapolis. She held this position for eighteen years.

Ms. Wright resides in Indianapolis, where she continues to relate to widows and their challenges as well as pursue her interests in read -ing, traveling, theatre, music and genealogy. Her web site is: www.TheWidowsJourney.com.

Bibliography

Berry, Mary Ellen and Carmen Renee Berry. *Reawakening to Life*. New York: The Crossroad Publishing Company, 2002.

Brooks, PH.D, Sam Goldstein, PH.D . *The Power of Resilience*. New York: McGraw Hill, 2003.

Caine, Lynn: *Being a Widow*. New York: Penguin Books, 1990.

Carlson, Richard, Ph.D. *You Can Be Happy No Matter What*. California: New World Library, 1997.

Chodron, Pema. *When Things Fall Apart*. Boston: Shambhala, 2000.

Chopra, Deepak. *The Seven Spiritual Laws of Success*. New World Library, 1993.

Davies, Paul, PH.D. *"That Mysterious Flow."* Scientific American, September, 2002 (40-47).

Foehner, Charlotte, Carol Cozart. *The Widow's Handbook*. Colorado: Fulcrum, Inc., 1988.

Ford, Debbie. *The Right Questions*. New York: Harper Collins, 2003.

Frost, Nina H., Dr. Kenneth C. Ruge, Dr. Richard W. Shoup. *Soul Mapping*. New York: Marlowe and Company, 2000.

Gafni, Marc. *Soul Prints*. New York: Simon and Shuster, 2001.

Hanh, Thich Nhat. *The Miracle of Mindfulness*. California: Parallax Press, 1985.

Hanh: *Being Peace*. California: Parallax Press, 1996.

James, John W., Russell Friedman. *The Grief Recovery Handbook*. New York: Harper Collins, 1998.

Kornfield, Jack. *A Path With Heart*. New York: Batam Books, 1993.

Kubler-Ross, Elisabeth. *On Life After Death*. California: Celestial Arts, 1991.

Lama, Dalai. *Ethics for the New Millennium*. New York: Riverhead Books, 1999.

Leick, Nini, Marianne Davidsen-Nielsen. *Healing Pain*. New York: Routledge, 1996.

Mitsch, Raymond R., Lynn Brookside. *Grieving the Loss of Someone You Love*. Ann Arbor Michigan: Servant Publications, 1993,

O'Connor, Nancy, PH.D. *Letting Go With Love:* The Grieving Process. Tucson: La Mariposa Press, 1984.

Rich, Phil, Ed.D. *The Healing Journey Through Grief.* New York: John Wiley and Sons, Inc., 1999.

Sanders, Catherine M.. Grief: *The Mourning After*. New York: John Wiley and Sons, 1999.

Tatelbaum, Judy. *The Courage To Grieve*. New York: Harper and Row

Weil, Andrew, M.D. c.d. *"Eight Meditations for Optimum Health."* New York: Upaya, 1997.

Weil. CD. *"Sound body, sound mind: music for healing."* New York: Upaya, 1997.

Exercise 1

Make a list of things/activities you can do to be kinder to your body and spirit.

Exercise 2

Write below any feelings you have of regret. Acknowledge those that are valid. For those regrets that have no validity, acknowledge them as well. Now, write yourself a letter forgiving yourself for those things about which you feel regret. You're human, it's okay you were not always perfect. As for the regrets that have no validity, it's time to see them for what they are and get rid of them.

Exercise 3

Make a list of those problems you are having dealing with the outside world. Then, make a list of possible things you can do to make those encounters easier for you.

Exercise 4

Make a list of activities you used to enjoy and the people you enjoyed dong them with. Now, write down ways you can begin to slowly incorporate some of them back into your life.

Exercise 5

Pretend that you are seven years older than you are right no...
Write a letter to yourself from the perspective of seven years fro...
now. Tell yourself you are a valuable person who deserves to...
happy. Describe in your letter what you want your life to look like...
seven years and what you can do to move in that direction.

Made in the USA
Lexington, KY
17 March 2010